Parenting Crazy Teens

**Tips and Strategies
for**

Handling Difficult Teen Parenting Situations

Parenting Crazy Teens

**Tips and Strategies
for Handling Difficult Teen Parenting Situations**

The Best Parenting Style in a Digital World

By

Dr. Sarah Moore Davi

ISBN: 978-0-9866060-0-7 (Paperback)

ISBN: 978-0-9866060-1-4 (e-book)

Library and Archives Canada Cataloguing in Publication

Library of Congress Control Number: 2010905251

This publication is designed to provide accurate and authoritative information that is up-to-date and current at the time of this publication. It is published with the understanding that the publisher is not engaged in rendering any professional services, advise or recommendation.

Self-Help Publishers does not endorse any product or service or recommendation/advise in this publication. Any service or services provider listed in this publication assume full liability for their products, services , recommendation/advise and any claims direct or indirect arising from them.

Disclaimer

Some of the Content in this publication may have been compiled from a variety of sources and are subject to change without notice. Although every effort has been made to contact the copyright holders of materials by the authors/editors, if readers of this book consider materials to be their copyright and have not been contacted by the author/editors please contact the publisher.

All of the names and characters in this book are fictitious and any resemblance to actual person, alive or dead, purely coincidental.

Send your wholesale inquiries in U.S.A to Ingram Book Group, **Baker & Taylor, and Nacscorp.**
In United Kingdom and Europe send your wholesale inquiries to Bertram and Blackwell's.
For retail purchase visit your local Amazon and Barns and Nobles online bookstores or checkout with your local bookstore.

For reprint/co-publishing rights contact Self-Help Publishers at info@selfhelppublishers.com
Manufactured in United States of America and United Kingdom simultaneously
by arrangements with Self-Help publishers.

Making the decision to have a child is momentous. It is to decide forever to have your heart go walking around outside your body. ~Elizabeth Stone

Always kiss your children goodnight - even if they're already asleep. ~H. Jackson Brown, Jr.

To bring up a child in the way he should go, travel that way yourself once in a while. ~Josh Billings

Your children need your presence more than your presents. ~Jesse Jackson

Children are a great comfort in your old age - and they help you reach it faster, too. ~Lionel Kauffman

Children need love, especially when they do not deserve it. ~Harold Hulbert

If our American way of life fails the child, it fails us all. ~Pearl S. Buck

Like fruit, children are sweetest just before they turn bad. ~Dena Groquet

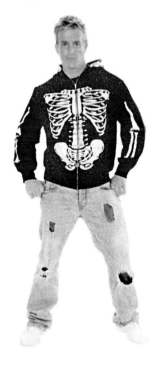

A WORD TO THE WISE

Don't forget to download e-book version of this book in pdf format to enjoy crisp clear color photos and active links.

So you can enjoy your reading on iPod, iPhone,PDA or on any hand held device. E-book is also low priced. Please check at www.ebookmall.com or any other e-book vender.

Table of Contents

Chapter 1

Chapter 2

Chapter 3

Chapter 4

Chapter 5

Chapter 6

Chapter 7

Chapter 8

Chapter 9

Chapter 10

Chapter 11

Chapter 12

Chapter 13

Chapter 14

Chapter 15

Index

Chapter 1

Surviving the Teen Years

You've lived through 2 AM feedings, toddler temper tantrums, and the back-to-school blues. So why is the word "teenager" causing you so much anxiety?

When you consider that the teen years are a period of intense growth, not only physically but morally and intellectually, it's understandable that it's a time of confusion and upheaval for many families.

Despite some adults' negative perceptions about teens, they are often energetic, thoughtful, and idealistic, with a deep interest in what's fair and right. So, although it can be a period of conflict between parent and

Best Parenting Style Today To Keep Your Family Together

child, the teen years are also a time to help kids grow into the distinct individuals they will become.

Best Parenting Style Today To Keep Your Family Together

Understanding the Teen Years

So when, exactly, does adolescence start? The message to send your kid is: Everybody's different. There are early bloomers, late arrivers, speedy developers, and slow-but-steady growers. In other words, there's a wide range of what's considered normal.

But it's important to make a (somewhat artificial) distinction between puberty and adolescence. Most of us think of puberty as the development of adult sexual characteristics: breasts, menstrual periods, pubic hair, and facial hair. These are certainly the most visible signs of impending adulthood, but kids who are showing physical changes (between the ages of 8 and 14 or so) can also be going through a bunch of changes that aren't readily seen from the outside. These are the changes of adolescence.

Many kids announce the onset of adolescence with a dramatic change in behavior around their parents. They're starting to separate from Mom and Dad and to become more independent. At the same time, kids this age are increasingly aware of how others, especially their peers, see them and are desperately trying to fit in.
Kids often start "trying on" different looks and identities, and they become acutely aware of how they differ from their peers, which can result in episodes of distress and conflict with parents.

Butting Heads

One of the common stereotypes of adolescence is the rebellious, wild teen continually at odds with Mom and Dad. Although it may be the case for some kids and this *is* a time of emotional ups and downs, that stereotype certainly is *not* representative of most teens.

But the primary goal of the teen years is to achieve independence. For this to occur, teens will start pulling away from their parents — especially the parent whom they're the closest to. This can come across as teens always seeming to have different opinions than their parents or not wanting to be around their parents in the same way they used to.

As teens mature, they start to think more abstractly and rationally. They're forming their moral code. And parents of teens may find that kids who previously had been willing to conform to please them will suddenly begin asserting themselves — and their opinions — strongly and rebelling against parental control.

You may need to look closely at how much room you give your teen to be an individual and ask yourself questions such as: "Am I a controlling parent?," "Do I listen to my child?," and "Do I allow my child's opinions and tastes to differ from my own?"

15 Dazzling Hollywood Teen Stars

Tips for Parenting During the Teen Years

Looking for a roadmap to find your way through these years? Here are some tips:

Educate Yourself

Read books about teenagers. Think back on your own teen years. Remember your struggles with acne or your embarrassment at developing early — or late. Expect some mood changes in your typically sunny child, and be prepared for more conflict as he or she matures as an individual. Parents who know what's coming can cope with it better. And the more you know, the better you can prepare.

Best Parenting Style Today To Keep Your Family Together

Talk to Your Child Early Enough

Talking about menstruation or wet dreams after they've already started means you're too late. Answer the early questions kids have about bodies, such as the differences between boys and girls and where babies come from. But don't overload them with information — just answer their questions.

You know your kids. You can hear when your child's starting to tell jokes about sex or when attention to personal appearance is increasing. This is a good time to jump in with your own questions such as:

- Are you noticing any changes in your body?
- Are you having any strange feelings?
- Are you sad sometimes and don't know why?

A yearly physical exam is a great time to bring up these things. A doctor can tell your preadolescent — and you — what to expect in the next few years. An exam can serve as a jumping-off point for a good parent/child discussion. The later you wait to have this discussion, the more likely your child will be to form misconceptions or become embarrassed about or afraid of physical and emotional changes.

Furthermore, the earlier you open the lines of communication, the better chance you have of keeping them open through the teen years. Give your child books on puberty written for kids going through it. Share memories of your own adolescence. There's nothing like knowing that Mom or Dad went through it, too, to put a child more at ease.

Put Yourself in Your Child's Place

Practice empathy by helping your child understand that it's normal to be a bit concerned or self-conscious, and that it's OK to feel grown-up one minute and like a kid the next.

Pick Your Battles

If teenagers want to dye their hair, paint their fingernails black, or wear funky clothes, think twice before you object. Teens want to shock their parents and it's a lot better to let them do something temporary and harmless; leave the objections to things that really matter, like tobacco, drugs and alcohol.

Maintain Your Expectations

Teens will likely act unhappy with expectations their parents place on them. However, they usually understand and need to know that their parents care enough about them to expect certain things such as good grades, acceptable behavior, and adherence to the rules of the house. If parents have appropriate expectations, teens will likely try to meet them.

Inform Your Teen — and Stay Informed Yourself

The teen years often are a time of experimentation, and sometimes that experimentation includes risky behaviors. Don't avoid the subjects of sex, or drug, alcohol, and tobacco use; discussing these things openly with kids **before** they're exposed to them increases the chance that they'll act responsibly when the time comes.

Know your child's friends — and know their friends' parents. Regular communication between parents can go a long way toward creating a safe environment for all teens in a peer group. Parents can help each other keep track of the kids' activities without making the kids feel that they're being watched.

Know the Warning Signs

A certain amount of change may be normal during the teen years, but too drastic or long-lasting a switch in personality or behavior may signal real trouble — the kind that needs professional help. Watch for one or more of these warning signs:

- extreme weight gain or loss
- sleep problems

- rapid, drastic changes in personality
- sudden change in friends
- skipping school continually
- falling grades
- talk or even jokes about suicide
- signs of tobacco, alcohol, or drug use
- run-ins with the law

Any other inappropriate behavior that lasts for more than 6 weeks can be a sign of underlying trouble, too. You may expect a glitch or two in your teen's behavior or grades during this time, but your A/B student shouldn't suddenly be failing, and your normally outgoing kid shouldn't suddenly become constantly withdrawn. Your doctor or a local counselor, psychologist, or psychiatrist can help you find proper counseling.

Respect Kids' Privacy

Some parents, understandably, have a very hard time with this one. They may feel that anything their kids do is their business. But to help your teen become a young adult, you'll need to grant some privacy. If you notice warning signs of trouble, then you can invade your child's privacy until you get to the heart of the problem. But otherwise, it's a good idea to back off.

In other words, your teenager's room and phone calls should be private. You also shouldn't expect your teen to share all thoughts or activities with you at all times. Of course, for safety reasons, you should always know where teens are going, what they're doing, and with whom, but you don't need to know every detail. And you definitely shouldn't expect to be invited along!

Monitor What Kids See and Read

TV shows, magazines and books, the Internet — kids have access to tons of information. Be aware of what yours watch and read. Don't be afraid to set limits on the amount of time spent in front of the computer or the TV. Know what they're learning from the media and who they may be communicating with online.

Make Appropriate Rules

Bedtime for a teenager should be age appropriate, just as it was when your child was a baby. Reward your teen for being trustworthy. Does your child keep to a 10 PM curfew? Move it to 10:30 PM. And does a teen always have to go along on family outings? Decide what your expectations are, and don't be insulted when your growing child doesn't always want to be with you. Think back: You probably felt the same way about *your* mom and dad.

Will This Ever Be Over?

As kids progress through the teen years, you'll notice a slowing of the highs and lows of adolescence. And, eventually, they'll become independent, responsible, communicative young adults. So remember the motto of many parents with teens: We're going through this together, and we'll come out of it — together!

Best Parenting Style Today To Keep Your Family Together

Best Parenting Style Today To Keep Your Family Together

Chapter 2

Connecting With Your Preteen

As your child approaches the teen years and becomes more independent, staying connected may seem like more of a challenge. But it's as important as ever - maybe even more so now.

While activities at school, new interests, and a burgeoning social life become more important to your growing child, you are still home base, providing love, guidance, and support.

And that connection to you will provide a sense of security and build the resilience your child needs to roll with life's ups and downs.

Best Parenting Style Today To Keep Your Family Together

What to Expect

Your preteen may act as if your guidance isn't welcome or needed, and even seem embarrassed by you at times. This is when kids start to confide more in peers and request their space and privacy - expect the bedroom door to be shut more often.

As difficult as it may be to swallow all these changes, try not to take them personally. They're all signs of your child's growing independence. You're going to have to loosen the ties and allow some growing room. But you don't have to let go entirely. You're still a powerful influence - it's just that your preteen may be more responsive to the example you set rather than the instructions you give. So practice what you'd like to preach, just preach it a little less for now.

Modeling the qualities that you want your preteen to learn and practice - respectful communication, kindness, healthy eating, and fulfilling everyday responsibilities without complaining - makes it more likely that your son or daughter will comply.

What You Can Do

Small, simple things can reinforce connection. Make room in your schedule for special times, take advantage of the routines you already share, and show that you care.
Here are some tips:

- **Family Meals:** It may seem like drudgery to prepare a meal, particularly after a long day. But a shared family meal provides valuable together time. So schedule it and organize it just as you would any other activity. Even if you have to pick up something pre-made, sit down together to eat it. Turn off the TV and try to tune out the ringing phone. If it's impossible to do every night, schedule a regular weekly family dinner night that accommodates your child's schedule. Make it something fun, and get everyone involved in the preparation and the cleanup. Sharing an activity helps build closeness and connection, and everyone pitching in reinforces a sense of responsibility and teamwork.

- **Bedtime and Goodnight:** Your child may not need to be tucked in anymore, but maintaining a consistent bedtime routine helps your preteen get the sleep needed to grow healthy and strong. So work in some winding-down time together before the lights go out. Read together. Go over the highlights of the day and talk about tomorrow. And even if your preteen has outgrown the tuck-in routine, there's still a place for a goodnight kiss or hug. If it's shrugged off, try a gentle hand on the shoulder or back as you wish your child a good night's sleep.

- **Share Ordinary Time:** Find little things that let you just hang out together. Invite your preteen to come with you to walk the dog. Invite yourself along on his or her run. Washing the car, baking cookies, renting movies, watching a favorite TV show - all are opportunities to enjoy each other's company. And they're chances for your child to talk about what's on his or her mind. Even riding in the car is an opportunity to connect. When you're driving, your preteen may be more inclined to mention a troubling issue. Since you're focused on the road, he or she doesn't have to make eye contact, which can ease any discomfort about opening up.

- **Create Special Time:** Make a tradition out of celebrating family milestones beyond birthdays and holidays. Marking smaller occasions like a good report card or a winning soccer game helps reinforce family bonds.

- **Show Affection:** Don't underestimate the value of saying and showing how much you love your preteen. Doing so ensures that your child feels secure and loved. And you're demonstrating healthy ways of showing affection. That said, your son or daughter may start to feel self-conscious about big displays of affection from you, especially in public. Your child may pull away from your hug and kiss, but it's not about you. Just reserve this type of affection for times when friends aren't around. And in public, find other ways to show that you care. A smile or a wave can convey a warm send-off while respecting boundaries.

Recognize out loud your child's wonderful qualities and developing skills when you see them. You might say, "That's a beautiful drawing - you're really very artistic" or "You were amazing at baseball practice today - I loved watching you out there."

- **Stay Involved:** Stay involved in your preteen's expanding pursuits. Getting involved gives you more time together and shared experiences. You don't have to be the Scout leader, homeroom mom, or soccer coach to be involved. And your child may want to do more activities where you're not in charge. That's OK. Go to games and practices when you can; when you can't, ask how things went and listen attentively. Help your child talk through the disappointments, and be sympathetic about the missed fly ball that won the game for the other team. Your attitude about setbacks will teach your preteen to accept and feel OK about them, and to summon the courage to try again.

- **Stay Interested:** Stay interested and curious about your preteen's ideas, feelings, and experiences. If you listen to what he or she is saying, you'll get a better sense of the guidance, perspective, and support needed. And responding in a nonjudgmental way means your child will be more likely to come to you anytime tough issues arise.

Best Parenting Style Today To Keep Your Family Together

"Your mother and I are not happy about your BLOG's criticism of our parenting skills."

Best Parenting Style Today To Keep Your Family Together

Talking to Your Child About Puberty

Today, kids are exposed to so much information about sex and relationships on TV and the Internet that by the time they approach puberty, they may be familiar with some advanced ideas. And yet, talking about the issues of puberty remains an important job for parents because not all of a child's information comes from reliable sources.

Don't wait for your child to come to you with questions about his or her changing body — that day may never arrive, especially if your child doesn't know it's OK talk to you about this sensitive topic.

Timing is Everything

Ideally, as a parent, you've already started talking to your child about the changes our bodies go through as we grow. Since the toddler years,kids have questions and most of your discussions probably come about as the result of your child's inquiries.

It's important to answer these questions about puberty honestly and openly — but don't always wait for your child to initiate a discussion. By the time kids are 8 years old, they should know what physical and emotional changes are associated with puberty. That may seem young, but consider this: some girls are wearing training bras by then and some boys begin to grow facial hair just a few years later.

With girls, it's vital that parents talk about menstruation before they actually get their periods. If they are unaware of what's happening, girls can be frightened by the sight and location of blood. Most girls get their first period when they're 12 or 13 years old, although some get it as early as age 8 and others get it as late as age 16.

On average, boys begin going through puberty a little later than girls, usually around age 11 or 12. But they may begin to develop sexually or have their first ejaculation without looking older or developing facial hair first.

Just as it helps adults to know what to expect with changes such as moving to a new home or working for a new company, kids should know about puberty beforehand.

Many kids receive some sex education at school. Often, though, the lessons are segregated, and the girls hear primarily about menstruation and training bras while the boys hear about erections and changing voices. It's important that girls learn about the changes boys go through and that boys learn about those affecting girls, so check with teachers about their lesson plans so you know what gaps need to be filled.

What to Say

When talking to kids about puberty, it's important to offer reassurance that these changes are normal. Puberty brings about so many changes, and it's easy for a child to feel insecure.

Many times, adolescents will express insecurity about their appearance as they go through puberty, but it can help them to know that everyone goes through the same things and that there's a huge amount of normal variation in their timing. Acne, mood changes, growth spurts, and hormonal changes — it's all part of growing up and everyone goes through it, but not always at the same pace.

Girls may begin puberty as early as second or third grade, and it can be upsetting if your daughter is the first one to get a training bra, for example. She may feel alone and awkward or like all eyes are on her in the school locker room.

With boys, observable changes include the deepening of the voice and the growth of facial hair. And just as with girls, if your son is an early bloomer, he may feel awkward or like he's the subject of stares from his classmates.

Kids should know the following about puberty:
- Girls become more rounded, especially in the hips and legs.
- Girls' breasts begin to swell and then grow.
- Girls and boys get pubic hair and underarm hair, and their leg hair becomes thicker and darker.
- Boys' penises and testicles grow larger.
- Boys' voices change and become deeper.
- Boys sometimes have wet dreams, which means they ejaculate in their sleep.
- When a girl begins menstruating, once a month, her uterine lining fills with blood in preparation for a fertilized egg. If the egg isn't

fertilized, she will have a period. If it is fertilized, she will become pregnant.

- A girl's period may last 3 days to a week, and she can use sanitary napkins (pads) or tampons to absorb the blood.

Best Parenting Style Today To Keep Your Family Together

Best Parenting Style Today To Keep Your Family Together

Common Questions

Not surprisingly, kids usually have lots of questions as they learn about puberty. For you, it's important to make sure you give your child the time and opportunity to ask questions — and answer them as honestly and thoroughly as possible.

Some of the most common questions are:

Questions	Answers
What is this hard lump in my breast?	Girls may notice small, sometimes tender, lumps beneath their nipples as their breasts are beginning to develop. This is perfectly normal. The firmness and tenderness will go away in time as the breasts continue to enlarge.
Why are my breasts so small (or so large)?	Breast size is hereditary, and your daughter needs to be reassured that, big or small, all breasts are beautiful. Size won't affect your daughter's attractiveness or her ability to breastfeed if she becomes a mother someday.
Why is my penis so small (or so large)?	With boys, the focus can be on the penis. It's important to reassure your son that the size of the penis when erect has nothing to do with the size of the penis when it's not.
Why don't I have pubic hair yet?	Everyone develops pubic hair, although some teens are hairier than others and some get it later than others. Just as with breast size or height, the amount or thickness of pubic hair is an individual trait.
I'm a boy, so why am I getting breasts?	Some boys experience temporary breast growth during puberty. The condition, called gynecomastia, is caused by some hormones produced by the testicles during puberty. It usually disappears, often within a few months to 1 year.
Why haven't I gotten my period yet?	As with all of the changes in puberty, periods come at different times for different girls. Some girls may not get their periods until they are 16 years old. This is usually normal, although it can be tough for them when all of their friends have already gotten their periods.

Tips for Talking

Let your child know that you're available any time to talk, but it's also important that you make time to talk. Just as it can be embarrassing or difficult for you to talk about these sensitive topics, your child may hesitate to go to you. As a parent, it's your job to try to discuss puberty

— and the feelings associated with those changes — as openly as possible.

It can be made easier if you're confident that you know the subject matter. First, before you answer your child's questions, make sure your own questions about puberty have been answered. If you're not entirely comfortable having a conversation about puberty, practice what you want to say first or ask your child's teacher for advice. Let your child know that it's a little uncomfortable for you, but it's an important talk to have.

If there are questions or concerns about pubertal development that you can't answer, a visit to your child's doctor may help provide reassurance.

Best Parenting Style Today To Keep Your Family Together

Chapter 3

Understanding Puberty

Your daughter is asking about getting her first bra, and your son comes home from soccer practice smelling like he's been digging on a road crew all day. What's going on?

Welcome to puberty, the time when kids sprout up, fill out, and maybe even mouth off.

Puberty was awkward enough when **you** were the one going through it. So how can you help your child through all the changes?

Stages of Puberty

Sure, most of us know the telltale signs of puberty — hair growth in new places, menstruation, body odor, lower voice in boys, breast growth in girls, etc. But we may not fully comprehend the science behind all of these changes. Here's a quick look at how it works.

Usually after a girl's 8th birthday or after a boy turns 9 or 10, puberty begins when an area of the brain called the hypothalamus starts to release gonadotropin-releasing hormone (GnRH). When GnRH travels to the pituitary gland (a small gland under the brain that produces hormones that control other glands throughout the body), it releases two more puberty hormones — luteinizing hormone (LH) and follicle-stimulating hormone (FSH).

What happens next depends on gender:

- **Boys:** Hormones travel through the bloodstream to the testes (testicles) and give the signal to begin production of sperm and the hormone testosterone.
- **Girls:** Hormones go to the ovaries (the two oval-shaped organs that lie to the right and left of the uterus) and trigger the maturation and release of eggs and the production of the hormone estrogen, which matures a female's body and prepares her for pregnancy.

At about the same time, the adrenal glands of both boys and girls begin to produce a group of hormones called adrenal androgens. These hormones stimulate the growth of pubic and underarm hair in both sexes.

For a Boy

The physical changes of puberty for a boy usually start with enlargement of the testicles and sprouting of pubic hair, followed by a growth spurt between ages 10 and 16 — on average 1 to 2 years later than when girls start. His arms, legs, hands, and feet also grow faster than the rest of his body. His body shape will begin to change as his shoulders broaden and he gains weight and muscle.

A boy may become concerned if he notices tenderness or swelling under his nipples. This temporary development of breast tissue is called gynecomastia and it happens to about 50% of boys during puberty. But it usually disappears within 6 months or so.
And that first crack in the voice is a sign that his voice is changing and will become deeper.

Dark, coarse, curly hair will also sprout just above his penis and on his scrotum, and later under his arms and in the beard area. His penis and testes will get larger, and erections, which a boy begins experiencing as an infant, will become more frequent. Ejaculation — the release of sperm-containing semen — will also occur.
Many boys become concerned about their penis size. A boy may need reassurance, particularly if he tends to be a later developer and he compares himself with boys who are further along in puberty. If a boy is circumcised, he may also have questions about the skin that covers the tip of an uncircumcised penis.

For a Girl

Puberty generally starts earlier for girls, some time between 8 and 13 years of age. For most girls, the first evidence of puberty is breast development, but it can be the growth of pubic hair. As her breasts start to grow, a girl will initially have small, firm, tender lumps (called buds) under one or both nipples; the breast tissue will get larger and become less firm in texture over the next year or two. Dark, coarse, curly hair will appear on her labia (the folds of skin surrounding the vagina), and later, similar hair will begin growing under her arms.

The first signs of puberty are followed 1 or 2 years later by a noticeable growth spurt. Her body will begin to build up fat, particularly in the breasts and around her hips and thighs, as she takes on the contours of a woman. Her arms, legs, hands, and feet will also get bigger.

The culminating event will be the arrival of menarche, her first period (menstruation). Depending on the age at which they begin their pubertal development, girls may get their first period between the ages of 9 and 16.

Best Parenting Style Today To Keep Your Family Together

Common Puberty Concerns

The physical changes kids experience as they move toward adulthood often are accompanied by emotional consequences.

Some girls are excited about their budding breasts and new training bras; others may worry that all eyes are focused on their breasts. Some boys love the sight of themselves all lathered up with shaving cream; others may be uncomfortable with the attention they get for a few new shoots of hair.

Pimples are common for most teens. Acne is caused by glands in the skin that produce a natural oil called sebum. Puberty hormones make the glands produce extra sebum, which can clog the pores. Washing gently with water and mild soap can get rid of excess sebum and help reduce breakouts.

Over-the-counter and prescription medications are available for more severe cases of acne. Your family doctor can recommend a dermatologist (a doctor specializing in skin) if basic skin care and OTC medications don't keep acne under control.

Kids who once associated bath time with play need to learn to wash regularly and to apply deodorant or antiperspirant. A teen who's learning to use shave will need instructions on how to keep it clean, to throw a disposable one away before it becomes dull and ineffective, and to not share it with others.

Boys, capable of having erections since infancy, can now experience ejaculation. The first ejaculation usually occurs between the ages of 11 and 15, either spontaneously in connection with sexual fantasies, during masturbation, or as a nocturnal emission (also called a wet dream). If he doesn't know about wet dreams before he has one, a boy may think he has urinated accidentally or that something has gone wrong with his body.

As kids mature physically and emotionally, they become increasingly curious about their sexuality and their own bodies. Although infants and younger children do touch their own genitals from time to time because they like the way it feels, masturbation is more common in older kids, from the preadolescent and teen years and beyond.

As far as the myths and beliefs about masturbation: No ... it won't cause kids to grow hair on their hands, become infertile, go blind, or develop new emotional problems. A small number of kids and teens with *already existing* emotional problems may become preoccupied with masturbation — just as they may become overly occupied with other behaviors or thoughts. Constant or obsessive masturbation may be a sign of anxiety or other emotional problem.

But, other than that, masturbation is generally considered by doctors to be a common form of normal sexual self-exploration. Although some preteens and teens may choose to masturbate, others may not.

Because masturbation is often considered a private topic, many kids might feel too embarrassed to talk about it because they're concerned that their parents will be angry or disappointed with them. Some kids may prefer to talk to older siblings, friends, or their doctors than a parent. If you continue to be concerned or have questions about masturbation, consult your doctor.

Talking to Kids About Puberty

Boys and girls can see these changes happening to each other — in some cases, they can smell them. It's important to talk to your child about how bodies change — sooner, rather than later.

Be prepared to talk to a girl about the expected events of puberty, including menstruation, when you see the first signs of breast development, or earlier if she seems ready or has questions. A boy should know about normal penile development, erections, and nocturnal emissions before age 12 — sooner, if he's an early developer. And it's also important to talk to your child about what's happening to members of the opposite sex.

It's best not to have "The Talk" as one grand summit but rather as a series of talks, ideally beginning when your child is young and starting to ask questions about body parts. Each time you talk, offer more and more detail, depending upon your child's maturity level and interest in the topic.

And, if your child has a question, answer it honestly. If you feel uncomfortable, need answers to questions, or are uncertain about how to have these talks with your child, ask your doctor for advice.

Best Parenting Style Today To Keep Your Family Together

Chapter 4

Kids and Alcohol

As much as parents may not like to think about it, the truth is that many kids and teens try alcohol during their high school and college years, long before it's legal for them to drink it. Research has shown that nearly 80% of high school kids have tried alcohol.

Although experimentation with alcohol may be common among kids, it's not safe or legal. So it's important to start discussing alcohol use and abuse with your kids at an early age and keep talking about it as they grow up.

The Effects of Alcohol Abuse

Alcohol interferes with a person's perception of reality and ability to make good decisions. This can be particularly hazardous for kids and teens who have less problem-solving and decision-making experience. Short-term effects of drinking include:

- distorted vision, hearing, and coordination
- altered perceptions and emotions
- impaired judgment, which can lead to accidents, drowning, and other risky behaviors like unsafe sex and drug use
- bad breath
- hangovers

Long-term effects include:

- cirrhosis and cancer of the liver
- loss of appetite
- serious vitamin deficiencies
- stomach ailments
- heart and central nervous system damage
- memory loss
- an increased risk of impotence
- high risk for overdosing

Talking to Kids About Alcohol

Long before your kids are presented with a chance to drink alcohol, you can increase the chances that they'll just say "no."
Childhood is a time of learning and discovery, so it's important to encourage kids to ask questions, even ones that might be hard to answer. Open, honest, age-appropriate communication now sets the stage for your kids to come to you later with other difficult topics or problems.

Preschoolers

Although 3- and 4-year-olds aren't ready to learn the facts about alcohol or other drugs, they start to develop the decision-making and problem-solving skills they will need later on. You can help them develop those skills in some simple ways.

For instance, let toddlers choose their own clothing and don't worry if the choices don't match. This lets them know you think they're capable of making good decisions. Assign simple tasks and let kids know what a big help they are.

And set a good example of the behavior that you want your kids to demonstrate. This is especially true in the preschool years when kids tend to imitate adults' actions as a way of learning. So, by being active, eating healthy, and drinking responsibly, parents teach their kids important lessons early on.

Ages 4 to 7

Kids this age still think and learn mostly by experience and don't have a good understanding of things that will happen in the future. So keep discussions about alcohol in the present tense and relate them to things that kids know and understand. For example, watching TV with your child can provide a chance to talk about advertising messages. Ask about the ads you see and encourage kids to ask questions too.
Kids are interested in how their bodies work, so this is a good time to talk about maintaining good health and avoiding substances that might harm the body. Talk about how alcohol hurts a person's ability to see,

hear, and walk without tripping; it alters the way people feel; and it makes it hard to judge things like whether the water is too deep or if there's a car coming too close. And it gives people bad breath and a headache!

Best Parenting Style Today To Keep Your Family Together

Ages 8 to 11

The later elementary school years are a crucial time in which you can influence your child's decisions about alcohol use. Kids at this age tend to love to learn facts, especially strange ones, and are eager to learn how things work and what sources of information are available to them.

So it's a good time to openly discuss facts about alcohol: its long- and short-term effects and consequences, its physical effects, and why it's especially dangerous for growing bodies.

Kids also can be heavily influenced by friends now. Their interests may be determined by what their peers think. So teach your child to say "no" to peer pressure, and discuss the importance of thinking and acting as an individual.

Casual discussions about alcohol and friends can take place at the dinner table as part of your normal conversation: "I've been reading about young kids using alcohol. Do you ever hear about kids using alcohol or other drugs in your school?"

Ages 12 to 17

By the teen years, your kids should know the facts about alcohol and your attitudes and beliefs about substance abuse. So use this time to reinforce what you've already taught them and focus on keeping the lines of communication open.

Teens are more likely to engage in risky behaviors, and their increasing need for independence may make them want to defy their parents' wishes or instructions. But if you make your teen feel accepted and respected as an individual, you increase the chances that your child will try to be open with you.

Kids want to be liked and accepted by their peers, and they need a certain degree of privacy and trust. Avoid excessive preaching and threats, and instead, emphasize your love and concern. Even when they're annoyed by parental interest and questions, teens still recognize that it comes with the territory.

Teaching Kids to Say "No"

Teach kids a variety of approaches to deal with offers of alcohol:

- Encourage them to ask questions. If a drink of any kind is offered, they should ask, "What is it?" and "Where did you get it?"
- Teach them to say "no, thanks" when the drink offered is an alcoholic one.
- Remind them to leave any uncomfortable situation. Make sure they have money for transportation or a phone number where you or another responsible adult can be reached.
- Teach kids never to accept a ride from someone who has been drinking. Some parents find that offering to pick up their kids from an uncomfortable situation — no questions asked — helps encourage kids to be honest and call when they need help.

Risk Factors

Times of transition, such as the onset of puberty or a parents' divorce, can lead kids to alcohol use. So teach your kids that even when life is upsetting or stressful, drinking alcohol as an escape can make a bad situation much worse.

Kids who have problems with self-control or low self-esteem are more likely to abuse alcohol. They may not believe that they can handle their problems and frustrations without using something to make them feel better.

Kids without a sense of connectedness with their families or who feel different in some way (appearance, economic circumstances, etc.) may also be at risk. Those who find it hard to believe in themselves desperately need the love and support of parents or other family members.

In fact, not wanting to harm the relationships between themselves and the adults who care about them is the most common reason that young people give for not using alcohol and other drugs.

Best Parenting Style Today To Keep Your Family Together

General Tips

Fortunately, parents can do much to protect their kids from using and abusing alcohol:

- Be a good role model. Consider how your use of alcohol or medications may influence your kids. Consider offering only nonalcoholic beverages at parties and other social events to show your kids that you don't need to drink to have fun.
- Educate yourself about alcohol so you can be a better teacher. Read and collect information that you can share with kids and other parents.
- Try to be conscious of how you can help build your child's self-esteem. For example, kids are more likely to feel good about themselves if you emphasize their strengths and positively reinforce healthy behaviors.
- Teach kids to manage stress in healthy ways, such as by seeking help from a trusted adult or engaging in a favorite activity.

Recognizing the Signs

Despite your efforts, your child may still use — and abuse — alcohol. How can you tell? Here are some common warning signs:

- the odor of alcohol
- sudden change in mood or attitude
- change in attendance or performance at school
- loss of interest in school, sports, or other activities
- discipline problems at school
- withdrawal from family and friends
- secrecy
- association with a new group of friends and reluctance to introduce them to you
- alcohol disappearing from your home
- depression and developmental difficulties

It's important not to jump to conclusions based on only one or two signs. Adolescence is a time of change — physically, socially, emotionally, and intellectually. This can lead to erratic behavior and mood swings as kids try to cope with all of these changes.

Best Parenting Style Today To Keep Your Family Together

If your child is using alcohol, there will usually be a cluster of these signs, like changes in friends, behavior, dress, attitude, mood, and grades. If you see a number of changes, look for all explanations by talking to your kids, but don't overlook substance abuse as a possibility.

Other tips to try:

- Keep tabs on where your kids go.

- Know the parents of your child's friends.

- Always make sure you have a phone number where you can reach your child.

- Have kids check in regularly when they're away from home.

- When spending an extended length of time away from you, your child should check in periodically with a phone call, e-mail, or visit home.

For teens, especially those old enough to drive, consider negotiating and signing a behavioral contract. This contract should spell out the way you expect your child to behave and state the consequences if your teen drives under the influence. Follow through and take the keys away, if necessary.

Make part of the deal with your teen that you and the rest of your family also agree never to drink and drive. Also encourage responsible behaviors, such as planning for a designated driver or calling an adult for help rather than driving under the influence.

It's important to keep communication open and expectations reasonable. Tying responsible actions to freedoms such as a later curfew or a driver's license can be a powerful motivator. Teach your kids that freedom only comes with responsibility — a lesson that should last a lifetime.

Talking to Your Child About Drugs

Just as you inoculate your children against illnesses like measles, you can help "immunize" them against drug use by giving them the facts before they're in a risky situation.

When kids don't feel comfortable talking to parents, they're likely to seek answers elsewhere, even if their sources are unreliable. Kids who aren't properly informed are at greater risk of engaging in unsafe behaviors and experimenting with drugs.

Parenting
just like running a country

Best Parenting Style Today To Keep Your Family Together

What Should I Say to My Child?

Preschool to Age 7

Before you get anxious about talking to young kids, take heart. You've probably already laid the groundwork for a discussion. For instance, whenever you give a fever medication or an antibiotic to your child, you have the opportunity to discuss the benefits and the appropriate and responsible use of those drugs. This is also a time when your child is likely to be very attentive to your behavior and any guidance that you provide.

Start taking advantage of "teachable moments" now. If you see a character on a billboard or on TV with a cigarette, talk to your child about smoking, nicotine addiction, and what smoking does to person's body. This can lead into a discussion about other drugs and how they can potentially cause harm.

Keep the tone of these discussions calm and use terms that your child can understand. Be specific about the effects of the drugs: how they make a person feel, the risk of overdose, and the other long-term damage they can cause. To give your kids these facts, you might have to do a little research.

Ages 8 to 12

As your kids grow older, you can begin conversations with them by asking them what they think about drugs. By asking the questions in a nonjudgmental, open-ended way, you're more likely to get an honest response.

Kids this age usually are still willing to talk openly to their parents about touchy subjects. Establishing a dialogue now helps keep the door open as kids get older and are less inclined to share their thoughts and feelings so openly.

Even if your question doesn't immediately result in a discussion, you'll get your kids thinking about the issue. If you show your kids that you're willing to discuss the topic and hear what they have to say, they might be more willing to come to you for help in the future.

News, such as steroid use in professional sports, can be springboards for casual conversations about current events. Use these discussions to provide your kids with information about the risks of drugs.

Best Parenting Style Today To Keep Your Family Together

Ages 13 to 17

At this age, your kids are likely to know other kids who use or abuse alcohol or drugs. They're also likely to have friends and peers who drive. It's important to talk about the dangers of driving under the influence. Talk about the legal issues — jail time and fines — and the possibility that they or someone else might be killed or seriously injured.

Consider establishing a written or verbal contract on the rules about going out or using the car. You can promise to pick your kids up at any time (even 2:00 AM!) without asking questions if they call you when the person responsible for driving has been drinking or using drugs.

The contract also can detail other situations: For example, if you find out that someone drank or used drugs in your car while your son or daughter was behind the wheel, you may want to suspend driving privileges for 6 months. By discussing all of this with your kids from the start, you eliminate surprises and make your expectations clear.

Laying Good Groundwork

No parent, child, or family is immune to the effects of drugs. Some of the best kids can end up in trouble, even when they have made an effort to avoid it and even when they have been given the proper guidance from their parents.

However, certain groups of kids may be more likely to use drugs than others. Kids who have friends who use drugs are likely to try drugs themselves. Those feeling socially isolated for whatever reason may turn to drugs. So it's important to know your child's friends — and their parents. Be involved in your children's lives. If your child's school runs an antidrug program, get involved. You might learn something! Pay attention to how your kids are feeling and let them know that you are available and willing to listen in a nonjudgmental way. Recognize when your kids are going through difficult times so that you can provide the support they need or seek additional care if it's needed.

A warm, open family environment — where kids are encouraged to talk about their feelings, where their achievements are praised, and where their self-esteem is bolstered — encourages kids to come forward with their questions and concerns. When censored in their own homes, kids go elsewhere to find support and answers to their most important questions.

Best Parenting Style Today To Keep Your Family Together

Chapter 5

Kids and Smoking

The health risks of tobacco are well known, yet the rates of smoking and the use of chewing tobacco continue to grow. Many people pick up these habits when they're young — in fact, 90% of all adult smokers started when they were kids. And each day, more than 4,400 kids become regular smokers.

Best Parenting Style Today To Keep Your Family Together

So it's important to make sure kids understand the dangers that go along with tobacco use. Smoking is the leading cause of preventable deaths in the United States. It can cause cancer, heart disease, and lung disease. Chewing tobacco (smokeless or spit tobacco) can lead to nicotine addiction, oral cancer, gum disease, and an increased risk of cardiovascular disease, including heart attacks.

Giving kids information about the risks of smoking and chewing tobacco, and establishing clear rules and your reasons for them, can help protect them from these unhealthy habits.

You should also know the warning signs of tobacco use and constructive ways to help someone kick the habit.

Best Parenting Style Today To Keep Your Family Together

The Facts About Tobacco

One of the major problems with smoking and chewing tobacco has to do with the chemical nicotine. A person can get addicted to nicotine within days of a first encounter with it. In fact, the nicotine in tobacco can be as addictive as cocaine or heroine. Nicotine affects mood as well as the heart, lungs, stomach, and nervous system.

And there are other health risks. Short-term effects of smoking include coughing and throat irritation. Over time, more serious conditions may develop, including increases in heart rate and blood pressure, bronchitis, and emphysema.

Finally, numerous studies indicate that young smokers are more likely to experiment with marijuana, cocaine, heroin, or other illicit drugs.

Best Parenting Style Today To Keep Your Family Together

Preventing Kids From Picking Up the Habit

Kids might be drawn to smoking and chewing tobacco for any number of reasons — to look cool, act older, lose weight, win cool merchandise, seem tough, or feel independent. But parents can combat those draws and keep kids from trying — and getting addicted to — tobacco.

Establish a good foundation of communication with your kids early on to make it easier to work through tricky issues like tobacco use. Some guidelines to keep in mind:

- Discuss sensitive topics in a way that doesn't make kids fear punishment or judgment.

- Emphasize what kids do right rather than wrong. Self-confidence is a child's best protection against peer pressure.

- Encourage kids to get involved in activities that prohibit smoking, such as sports.

- Show that you value your kids' opinions and ideas.

- It's important to keep talking to kids about the dangers of tobacco use over the years. Even the youngest child can understand that smoking is bad for the body.

- Ask what kids find appealing — or unappealing — about smoking. Be a patient listener.

- Read, watch TV, and go to the movies with your kids. Compare media images with what happens in reality.

- Discuss ways to respond to peer pressure to smoke. Your child may feel confident simply saying "no." But also offer alternative responses such as "It will make my clothes and breath smell bad" or "I hate the way it makes me look."

- Encourage kids to walk away from friends who don't respect their reasons for not smoking.

- Explain how much smoking governs the daily life of kids who start doing it. How do they afford the cigarettes? How do they have money to pay for other things they want? How does it affect their friendships?

- Establish firm rules that exclude smoking and chewing tobacco from your house and explain why: Smokers smell bad, look bad, and feel bad, and it's bad for everyone's health.

-

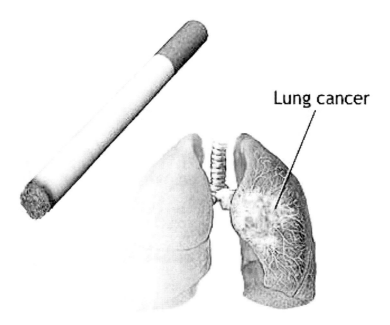

Lung cancer

If Your Child Smokes

If you smell smoke on your child's clothing, try not to overreact. Ask about it first — maybe your child has been hanging around with friends who smoke or just tried one cigarette. Many kids do try a cigarette at one time or another but don't go on to become regular smokers.
Additional signs of tobacco use include:

- coughing
- throat irritation
- hoarseness
- bad breath
- decreased athletic performance
- greater susceptibility to colds
- stained teeth and clothing (also signs of chewing tobacco use)
- shortness of breath

Sometimes even the best foundation isn't enough to stop kids from experimenting with tobacco. It may be tempting to get angry, but it's more productive to focus on communicating with your child.

Here are some tips that may help:

- Resist lecturing or turning your advice into a sermon.
- Uncover what appeals to your child about smoking and talk about it honestly.
- Many times, kids aren't able to appreciate how their current behaviors can affect their future health. So talk about the immediate downsides to smoking: less money to spend on other pursuits, shortness of breath, bad breath, yellow teeth, and smelly clothes.
- Stick to the smoking rules you've set up. And don't let a child smoke at home to keep the peace.

- If you hear, "I can quit any time I want," ask your child to show you by quitting cold turkey for a week.

- Try not to nag. Ultimately, quitting is your child's decision.

- Help your child develop a quitting plan and offer information and resources, and reinforce the decision to quit with praise.

- Stress the natural rewards that come with quitting: freedom from addiction, improved fitness, better athletic performance, and improved appearance.

- Encourage a meeting with your child's doctor, who can be supportive emotionally and may have treatment plans.

-

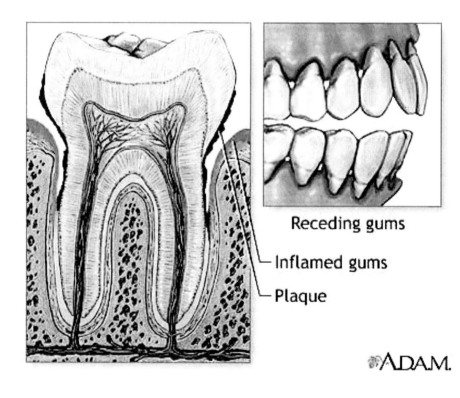

Receding gums

Inflamed gums

Plaque

ⒶADAM.

•

If You Smoke

Kids are quick to observe any contradiction between what their parents say and what they do. Despite what you might think, most kids say that the adult whom they most want to be like when they grow up is a parent. If you're a smoker:

- First, admit to that you made a mistake by starting to smoke and that if you had it to do over again, you'd never start.

- Second, quit. It's not simple and it may take a few attempts and the extra help of a program or support group. But your kids will be encouraged as they see you overcome your addiction to tobacco.

Reviewed by: Steven Dowshen, MD

Best Parenting Style Today To Keep Your Family Together

Chapter 6

Raising Confident Kids

It takes confidence to be a kid. Whether going to a new school or stepping up to bat for the first time, kids face a lot of uncharted territory.

Naturally, parents want to instill a can-do attitude in their kids so that they'll bravely take on new challenges and, over time, believe in themselves. While each child is a little different, parents can follow some general guidelines to build kids' confidence.

Self-confidence rises out of a sense of competence. In other words, kids develop confidence not because parents tell them they're great, but because of their achievements, big and small. Sure, it's good to hear encouraging words from mom and dad. But words of praise mean more when they refer to a child's specific efforts or new abilities.

When kids achieve something, whether it's brushing their own teeth or riding a bike, they get a sense of themselves as able and capable, and tap into that high-octane fuel of confidence.

Building self-confidence can begin very early. When babies learn to turn the pages of a book or toddlers learn to walk, they are getting the idea "I can do it!" With each new skill and milestone, kids can develop increasing confidence.

Parents can help by giving kids lots of opportunities to practice and master their skills, letting kids make mistakes and being there to boost their spirits so they keep trying. Respond with interest and excitement when kids show off a new skill, and reward them with praise when they achieve a goal or make a good effort.

With plentiful opportunities, good instruction, and lots of patience from parents, kids can master basic skills — like tying their shoes and making the bed. Then, when other important challenges present themselves, kids can approach them knowing that they have already been successful in other areas.

Best Parenting Style Today To Keep Your Family Together

Stay on the Sidelines

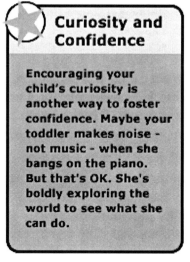

Curiosity and Confidence

Encouraging your child's curiosity is another way to foster confidence. Maybe your toddler makes noise - not music - when she bangs on the piano. But that's OK. She's boldly exploring the world to see what she can do.

Of course, supervision is important to ensure that kids stay safe. But to help them really learn a new skill, it's also important not to hover. Give kids the opportunity to try something new, make mistakes, and learn from them.

For instance, if your son wants to learn how to make a peanut butter sandwich, demonstrate, set up the ingredients, and let him give it a try. Will he make a bit of a mess? Almost certainly. But don't swoop in the second some jelly hits the countertop. In fact, avoid any criticism that could discourage him from trying again. If you step in to finish the sandwich, your son will think, "Oh well, I guess I can't make sandwiches."

But if you have patience for the mess and the time it takes to learn, the payoff will be real. Someday soon he'll be able to say, "I'm hungry for lunch, so I'm going to make my own sandwich." You might even reply, "Great, can you make me one, too?" What a clear sign of your faith in his abilities!

Best Parenting Style Today To Keep Your Family Together

Offer Encouragement and Praise

Sometimes, it won't be you swooping in when your child falters, but your child giving up. Help by encouraging persistence in the midst of frustration. By trying again, kids learn that obstacles can be overcome.
Once kids reach a goal, you'll want to praise not only the end result but also their willingness to stick with it. For instance, after your son has mastered making that peanut butter sandwich you might show your confidence by saying, "Next time, want to learn how to crack an egg?" Sandwich-fixing and egg-cracking might not seem like huge achievements, but they're important steps in the right direction — toward your child's independence.

Throughout childhood, parents have chances to prepare kids to take care of themselves. Sure, it's great to feel needed, but as kids steadily gain confidence and independence, their relationship with you can be even richer. You can be bonded, not just by dependence, but by love and shared pride in all they've achieved. Eventually, your grown-up kids just might say thanks for how prepared they feel for the road ahead — a road they can take with confidence.

Best Parenting Style Today To Keep Your Family Together

School Violence and the News

As terrible and frightening as incidents of school violence are, they are rare. Although it may not seem that way, the rate of crime involving physical harm has been declining at U.S. schools since the early 1990s.

According to the Centers for Disease Control and Prevention (CDC), fewer than 1% of all homicides among school-age children happen on school grounds or on the way to and from school. The vast majority of students will never experience violence at school or in college.

Still, it's natural for kids and teens — no matter where they go to school — to worry about whether this type of incident may someday affect them. How can you help them deal with these fears? Talking with kids about these tragedies, and what they watch or hear about them, can put frightening information into context.

Best Parenting Style Today To Keep Your Family Together

Talking to Your Kids

It's important for kids to feel like they can share their feelings, and know that their fears and anxieties are understandable.

Rather than waiting for your child to approach you, consider starting the conversation. Ask kids what they understand about these incidents and how they feel about them.

Share your own feelings too — during a tragedy, kids may look to adults for their reactions. It helps kids to know that they are not alone in their anxieties. Knowing that their parents have similar feelings will help kids legitimize their own.

At the same time, kids often need parents to help them feel safe. It may help to discuss in concrete terms what you have done and what the school is doing to help protect its students.

iPug

Best Parenting Style Today To Keep Your Family Together

What Schools Are Doing

Many schools are taking extra precautions to keep students safe. Some have focused on keeping weapons out by conducting random locker and bag checks, limiting entry and exit points at the school, and keeping the entryways under teacher supervision. Other schools use metal detectors.

Lessons on conflict resolution have been added to many schools' courses to help prevent troubled students from resorting to violence. Peer counseling and active peer programs help students become more aware of the signs that a fellow student may be becoming more troubled or violent.

Another thing that helps make schools safer is greater awareness of problems like bullying and discrimination. Many schools now have programs to fight these problems, and teachers and administrators know more about protecting students from violence.

How Kids Perceive the News

Of course, you are not your child's only source of information about school shootings or other tragic events that receive media attention. Kids are likely to repeatedly encounter news stories or graphic images on television, radio, or the Internet, and such reports can teach them to view the world as a confusing, threatening, or unfriendly place.

Unlike movies or entertainment programs, news is real. But depending on a child's age or maturity level, he or she may not yet understand the distinctions between fact and fantasy. By the time kids reach 7 or 8, however, what they watch on TV can seem all too real. For some youngsters, the vividness of a sensational news story can be internalized and transformed into something that might happen to them. A child watching a news story about a school shooting might worry, "Could I be next? Could that happen to me?" TV has the effect of shrinking the world and bringing it into our living rooms.

By concentrating on violent stories, TV news can also promote a "mean-world" syndrome that can give kids a misrepresentation of what the world and society are actually like.

Best Parenting Style Today To Keep Your Family Together

Best Parenting Style Today To Keep Your Family Together

Discussing the News

To calm fears about the news, parents should be prepared to deliver what psychologists call "calm, unequivocal, but limited information." This means delivering the truth, but in a way that fits the emotional level of your child. The key is to be truthful, but not go into more detail than your child is interested in or can handle.

Although it's true that some things can't be controlled, parents should still give kids the space to share their fears. Encourage them to talk openly about what scares them.

Older kids are less likely to accept an explanation at face value. Their budding skepticism about the news and how it's produced and sold might mask anxieties they have about the stories covered. If an older child is bothered about a story, help him or her cope with these fears. An adult's willingness to listen will send a powerful message.

Tips for Parents

Keeping an eye on what TV news kids watch can go a long way toward monitoring the content of what they hear and see about events like school shootings. Here are some additional tips:

- Recognize that news doesn't have to be driven by disturbing pictures. Public television programs, newspapers, or newsmagazines specifically designed for kids can be less sensational — and less upsetting — ways for them to get information.

- Discuss current events with your child on a regular basis. It's important to help kids think through stories they hear about. Ask questions: What do you think about these events? How do you think these things happen? Such questions can encourage conversation about non-news topics as well.

- Put news stories in proper context. Showing that certain events are isolated or explaining how one event relates to another helps kids make better sense of what they hear.

- Watch the news with your child to filter stories together.

- Anticipate when guidance will be necessary and avoid shows that aren't appropriate for your child's age or level of development.

- If you're uncomfortable with the content of the news or it's inappropriate for your child's age, turn it off.

Best Parenting Style Today To Keep Your Family Together

Chapter 7

Sibling Rivalry

"Dad, she's in my room getting into my things again!"

"Mom, he won't stop annoying me!"

"Me first! Me first! Me first!"

Sound familiar? If you have more than one child, the answer is probably "yes," because these are the sounds of sibling rivalry or sibling conflict.

While many kids are lucky enough to become the best of friends with their siblings, it's very common for brothers and sisters to fight. (It's also common for them to swing back and forth between adoring and detesting one other!)

Often, sibling rivalry starts even before the second child is born, and continues as the kids grow and compete for everything from toys to attention. As kids reach different stages of development, their evolving needs can significantly affect how they relate to one another.

It can be frustrating and upsetting to watch — and hear — your kids fight with one another. A household that's full of conflict is stressful for everyone. Yet often it's hard to know how to stop the fighting, and or even whether you should get involved at all. But you can take steps to promote peace in your household and help your kids get along.

Why Do My Kids Fight?

Many different things can cause siblings to fight. Most brothers and sisters experience some degree of jealousy or competition, and this can flare into squabbles and bickering. But other factors also might influence how often kids fight and how severe the fighting gets. These include:

- **Evolving needs.** It's natural for kids' changing needs, anxieties, and identities to affect how they relate to one another. For example, toddlers are naturally protective of their toys and belongings, and are learning to assert their will, which they'll do at every turn. So if a baby brother or sister picks up the toddler's toy, the older child may react aggressively. School-age kids often have a strong concept of fairness and equality, so might not

Best Parenting Style Today To Keep Your Family Together

understand why siblings of other ages are treated differently or feel like one child gets preferential treatment. Teenagers, on the other hand, are developing a sense of individuality and independence, and might resent helping with household responsibilities, taking care of younger siblings, or even having to spend time together. All of these differences can influence the way kids fight with one another.

- **Individual temperaments.** Your kids' individual temperaments — including mood, disposition, and adaptability — and their unique personalities play a large role in how well they get along. For example, if one child is laid back and another is easily rattled, they may often get into it. Similarly, a child who is especially clingy and drawn to parents for comfort and love might be resented by siblings who see this and want the same amount of attention.

Best Parenting Style Today To Keep Your Family Together

- **Special needs/sick kids.** Sometimes, a child's special needs due to illness or learning/emotional issues may require more parental time. Other kids may pick up on this disparity and act out to get attention or out of fear of what's happening to the other child.

- **Role models.** The way that parents resolve problems and disagreements sets a strong example for kids. So if you and your spouse work through conflicts in a way that's respectful, productive, and not aggressive, you increase the chances that your children will adopt those tactics when they run into problems with one another. If your kids see you routinely shout, slam doors, and loudly argue when you have problems, they're likely to pick up those bad habits themselves.

What Can I Do When the Fighting Starts?

While it may be common for brothers and sisters to fight, it's certainly not pleasant for anyone in the house. And a family can only tolerate a certain amount of conflict. So what should you do when the fighting starts?

Whenever possible, **don't get involved.** Step in only if there's a danger of physical harm. If you always intervene, you risk creating other problems. The kids may start expecting your help and wait for you to come to the rescue rather than learning to work out the problems on their own. There's also the risk that you — inadvertently — make it appear to one child that another is always being "protected," which could foster even more resentment. By the same token, rescued kids may feel that they can get away with more because they're always being "saved" by a parent.

If you're concerned by the language used or name-calling, it's appropriate to "coach" kids through what they're feeling by using appropriate words. This is different from intervening or stepping in and separating the kids.

Even then, encourage them to resolve the crisis themselves. If you do step in, try to resolve problems **with** your kids, not for them.

When getting involved, here are some steps to consider:

Best Parenting Style Today To Keep Your Family Together

- Separate kids until they're calm. Sometimes it's best just to give them space for a little while and not immediately rehash the conflict. Otherwise, the fight can escalate again. If you want to make this a learning experience, wait until the emotions have died down.

- Don't put too much focus on figuring out which child is to blame. It takes two to fight — anyone who is involved is partly responsible.

- Next, try to set up a "win-win" situation so that each child gains something. When they both want the same toy, perhaps there's a game they could play together instead.

Remember, as kids cope with disputes, they also learn important skills that will serve them for life — like how to value another person's perspective, how to compromise and negotiate, and how to control aggressive impulses.

Best Parenting Style Today To Keep Your Family Together

Helping Kids Get Along

Simple things you can do every day to prevent fighting include:

- Set ground rules for acceptable behavior. Tell the kids that there's no cursing, no name-calling, no yelling, no door slamming. Solicit their input on the rules — as well as the consequences when they break them. This teaches kids that they're responsible for their own actions, regardless of the situation or how provoked they felt, and discourages any attempts to negotiate regarding who was "right" or "wrong."

- Don't let kids make you think that everything always has to be "fair" and "equal" — sometimes one kid needs more than the other.

- Be proactive in giving your kids one-on-one attention directed to their interests and needs. For example, if one likes to go outdoors, take a walk or go to the park. If another child likes to sit and read, make time for that too.

- Make sure kids have their own space and time to do their own thing – to play with toys by themselves, to play with friends without a sibling tagging along, or to enjoy activities without having to share 50-50.

- Show and tell your kids that, for you, love is not something that comes with limits.

- Let them know that they are safe, important, and needed, and that their needs will be met.

- Have fun together as a family. Whether you're watching a movie, throwing a ball, or playing a board game, you're establishing a peaceful way for your kids to spend time together and relate to each other. This can help ease tensions between them and also keeps you involved. Since parental attention is something many kids fight over, fun family activities can help reduce conflict.

- If your children frequently squabble over the same things (such as video games or dibs on the TV remote), post a schedule showing which child "owns" that item at what times during the week. (But if they keep fighting about it, take the "prize" away altogether.)

- If fights between your school-age children are frequent, hold weekly family meetings in which you repeat the rules about fighting and review past successes in reducing conflicts. Consider establishing a program where the kids earn points toward a fun family-oriented activity when they work together to stop battling.

- Recognize when kids just need time apart from each other and the family dynamics. Try arranging separate play dates or activities for each kid occasionally. And when one child is on a play date, you can spend one-on-one time with another.

Keep in mind that sometimes kids fight to get a parent's attention. In that case, consider taking a time-out of your own. When you leave, the incentive for fighting is gone. Also, when your own fuse is getting short, consider handing the reins over to the other parent, whose patience may be greater at that moment.

Getting Professional Help

In a small percentage of families, the conflict between brothers and sisters is so severe that it disrupts daily functioning, or particularly affects kids emotionally or psychologically. In those cases, it's wise to get help from a mental health professional. Seek help for sibling conflict if it:

- is so severe that it's leading to marital problems

- creates a real danger of physical harm to any family member

- is damaging to the self-esteem or psychological well-being of any family member

- may be related to another psychiatric disorder, such as depression

If you have questions about your kids' fighting, talk with your doctor, who can help you determine whether your family might benefit from professional help and refer you to local mental health resources.

Best Parenting Style Today To Keep Your Family Together

Chapter 8

Sexual Attraction and Orientation

It's a natural part of life to have sexual feelings. As people pass from childhood, through adolescence, to adulthood, their sexual feelings develop and change.

During the teen years, sexual feelings are awakened in new ways because of the hormonal and physical changes of puberty. These changes involve both the body and the mind, and teens tend to wonder about new — and often intense — sexual feelings.
It takes time for many people to understand who they are and who they're becoming. Part of that understanding includes a person's sexual feelings and attractions.

The term **sexual orientation** refers to the gender (that is, male or female) to which a person is attracted. There are several types of sexual orientation that are commonly described:

- **Heterosexual.** People who are heterosexual are romantically and physically attracted to members of the opposite sex: Heterosexual males are attracted to females, and heterosexual females are attracted to males. Heterosexuals are sometimes called "straight."
- **Homosexual.** People who are homosexual are romantically and physically attracted to people of the same sex: Females who are attracted to other females are lesbian; males who are attracted to other males are often known as gay. (The term gay is sometimes also used to describe homosexual individuals of either gender.)
- **Bisexual.** People who are bisexual are romantically and physically attracted to members of both sexes.
-

Best Parenting Style Today To Keep Your Family Together

Teens — both boys and girls — often find themselves having sexual thoughts and attractions. For some, these feelings and thoughts can be intense — and even confusing or disturbing. That may be especially true for people who are having romantic or sexual thoughts about someone of the same gender. "What does that mean," they might think. "Am I gay?" Thinking sexually about both the same sex and the opposite sex is quite common as teens sort through their emerging sexual feelings. This type of imagining about people of the same or opposite sex doesn't necessarily mean that a person fits into a particular type of sexual orientation.

Some teens may also experiment with sexual experiences, including those with members of the same sex, during the years they are exploring their own sexuality. These experiences, by themselves, do not necessarily mean that a teen is gay or straight.

Do People Choose Their Sexual Orientation?

Most medical professionals, including organizations such as the American Academy of Pediatrics (AAP) and the American Psychological Association (APA), believe that sexual orientation involves a complex mixture of biology, psychology, and environmental factors. A person's genes and inborn

hormonal factors may play a role as well. These medical professionals believe that — in most cases — sexual orientation, whatever its causes, is not simply chosen.

Not everyone agrees. Some believe that individuals can choose who they are attracted to — and that people who are gay have chosen to be attracted to people of the same gender.

There are lots of opinions and stereotypes about sexual orientation. For example, having a more "feminine" appearance or interest does not mean that a teen boy is gay. And having a more "masculine" appearance doesn't mean a girl is lesbian. As with most things, making assumptions just based on looks can lead to the wrong conclusion.

It's likely that all the factors that result in someone's sexual orientation are not yet completely understood. What is certain is that people, no matter their sexual orientation, want to feel understood, respected, and accepted — particularly by their family. That's not always easy in every family.

What's It Like for Gay Teens?

For teens who are gay or lesbian, it can feel like everyone is expected to be straight. Because of this, some gay and lesbian teens may feel different from their friends when the heterosexual people around them start talking about romantic feelings, dating, and sex. They may feel like they have to pretend to feel things that they don't in order to fit. They might feel they need to deny who they are or that they have to hide an important part of themselves.

These feelings, plus fears of prejudice, can lead teens who aren't straight to keep their sexual orientation secret, even from friends and family who might be supportive. Kids and teens who are gay are likely to face people who express stereotypes, prejudices, and even hate about homosexuality.

Some gay or lesbian teens tell a few accepting, supportive friends and family members about their sexual orientation. This is often called **coming out**. Many lesbian, gay, and bisexual teens who come out to their friends and families are fully accepted by them and their communities. They feel comfortable about being attracted to someone of the same gender and don't feel particularly anxious about it.

But not everyone has the same feelings or good support systems. People who feel they need to hide who they are or who fear rejection, discrimination, or violence can be at greater risk for emotional problems like anxiety and depression.

Some gay teens without support systems can be at higher risk than heterosexual teens for dropping out of school, living on the streets, using alcohol and drugs, and even in some cases for attempting to harm themselves.

These difficulties are thought to happen more frequently not directly because they are gay, but because gay and lesbian people are more likely to be misunderstood, socially isolated, or mistreated because of their sexual orientation.

This doesn't happen to all gay teens, of course. Many gay and lesbian teens and their families have no more difficulties during the teen years than anyone else.

Best Parenting Style Today To Keep Your Family Together

The Importance of Talking

No matter what someone's sexual orientation is, learning about sexuality and relationships can be difficult for a teen to come to terms with. It can help a teen to talk to someone about the confusing feelings that go with growing up, whether it's a parent, another family member, a close friend or sibling, or a school counselor. It's not always easy for a teen to find somebody to talk to, but many of them find that confiding in someone they trust and feel close to, even if they're not completely sure how that person will react, turns out to be a positive experience.

In many communities, resources such as youth groups composed of teens who are facing similar issues can provide opportunities for people to talk to others who understand. Psychologists, psychiatrists, family doctors, and trained counselors can help teens cope — confidentially and privately — with the difficult feelings that go with their developing sexuality. These experts can also help teens to find ways to deal with any peer pressure, harassment, and bullying they may face. They can also help parents manage any complicated feelings they may be having as they come to terms with their teen's sexuality.

Whether gay, straight, bisexual, or just not sure, almost all teens have questions about reaching physical maturity and about sexual health (for example, avoiding sexually transmitted diseases). Because these can be difficult topics, it's especially important for gay and lesbian teens to find someone knowledgeable who they can trust and confide in.

Parents can help by becoming more knowledgeable about issues of sexuality — and learning to be more comfortable discussing them. Parents also can help their teen gain access to a doctor or health professional who will provide reliable health advice.

Chapter 9

Helping Teens Cope With Stress

Kids get to play and they don't have jobs, but they still have plenty to worry about. Stress from things like school and social situations can feel overwhelming for kids, particularly if they don't have healthy strategies to cope with strong feelings and solve everyday problems.

A recent KidsHealth® KidsPoll showed that kids deal with stress in both healthy and unhealthy ways, and while they may not initiate a conversation about what's bothering them, they do want their parents to reach out and help them cope with their feelings.

But it's not always easy for parents to know how to connect with a child who's feeling stressed.

Here are a few ideas:

Notice out loud. Tell your child when you notice something he or she might be feeling. ("It seems like you're still mad about what happened at the playground"). This shouldn't sound like an accusation (as in, "OK, what happened now? Are you still mad about that?") or put a child on the spot. It's just a casual observation that you're interested in hearing more about your child's concern.

Listen to your child. Ask your child to tell you what's wrong. Listen attentively and calmly — with interest, patience, openness, and caring. Avoid any urge to judge, blame, lecture, or say what you think your child should have done instead. The idea is to let your child's concerns (and feelings) be heard. Try to get the whole story by asking questions like "And then what happened?" Take your time. And let your child take his or her time, too.

Comment briefly on the feelings you think your child was experiencing. For example, you might say "That must have been upsetting," "No wonder you felt mad when they wouldn't let you in the game," or "That must have seemed unfair to you." Doing this shows that you understand what your child felt, why, and that you care. Feeling understood and listened to helps your child feel connected to you, and that is especially important in times of stress.

Put a label on it. Many kids do not yet have words for their feelings. If your child seems angry or frustrated, use those words to help him or her learn to identify the emotions by name. Putting feelings into words helps your child communicate and develop emotional awareness — the ability to recognize his or her own emotional states. A child who can do so is less likely to reach the behavioral boiling point where strong emotions get demonstrated through behaviors rather than communicated with words.

Best Parenting Style Today To Keep Your Family Together

Help your child think of things to do. Suggest activities your child can do to feel better now and to solve the problem at hand. Encourage your child to think of a couple of ideas. You can get the brainstorm started if necessary, but don't do all the work. Your child's active participation will build confidence. Support the good ideas and add to them as needed. Ask, "How do you think this will work?" Sometimes talking and listening and feeling understood is all that's needed to help a child's frustrations begin to melt away. Other times try changing the subject and moving on to something more positive and relaxing. Don't give the problem more attention than it deserves.

Just be there. Sometimes kids don't feel like talking about what's bothering them. Respect that, give your child space, and still make it clear that you'll be there when he or she does feel like talking. Even when kids don't communicate, they usually don't want parents to leave them alone. You can help your child feel better just by being there — keeping him or her company, spending time together. So if you notice that your child seems to be down in the dumps, stressed, or having a bad day — but doesn't feel like talking — initiate something you can do together. Take a walk, watch a movie, shoot some hoops, or bake some cookies. Isn't it nice to know that your presence really counts?

Be patient. As a parent, it hurts to see your child unhappy or worried. But try to resist the urge to fix every problem. Instead, focus on helping your child, slowly but surely, grow into a good problem-solver — a kid who knows how to roll with life's ups and downs, put feelings into words, calm down when needed, and bounce back to try again.

Remember that you can't fix everything, and that you won't be there to solve every problem as your child goes through life. But by teaching healthy coping strategies, you prepare your child to manage whatever stresses come in the future.

Best Parenting Style Today To Keep Your Family Together

Helping Teens Handle Worry

Kids don't have to pay bills, cook dinners, or manage carpools. But — just like adults — they have their share of daily demands and things that don't go smoothly. If frustrations and disappointments pile up, kids can get worried.

It's natural for all kids to worry at times, and because of personality and temperament differences, some may worry more than others. Luckily, parents can help kids manage worry and tackle everyday problems with ease. Kids who can do that develop a sense of confidence and optimism that will help them master life's challenges, big and small.

What Do Kids Worry About?

What kids worry about is often related to the age and stage they're in.

Kids and preteens typically worry about things like grades, tests, their changing bodies, fitting in with friends, that goal they missed at the soccer game, or whether they'll make the team. They may worry about social troubles like cliques, peer pressure, or whether they'll be bullied, teased, or left out.

Because they're beginning to feel more a part of the larger world around them, preteens also may worry about world events or issues they hear about on the news or at school. Things like terrorism, war, pollution, global warming, endangered animals, and natural disasters can become a source of worry.

Helping Kids Conquer Worry

To help your kids manage what's worrying them:

Find out what's on their minds: Be available and take an interest in what's happening at school, on the team, and with your kids' friends. Take casual opportunities to ask how it's going. As you listen to stories of the day's events, be sure to ask about what your kids think and feel about what happened.

If your child seems to be worried about something, ask about it. Encourage kids to put what's bothering them into words. Ask for key details and listen attentively. Sometimes just sharing the story with you can help lighten their load.

Show you care and understand. Being interested in your child's concerns shows they're important to you, too, and helps kids feel supported and understood. Reassuring comments can help — but usually only after you've heard your child out. Say that you understand your child's feelings and the problem.

Be sure to hear about the upbeat stuff, too. Give plenty of airtime to the good things that happen and let kids tell you what they think and feel about successes, achievements, and positive experiences.

Guide kids to solutions. You can help reduce worries by helping kids learn to deal constructively with challenging situations. When your child tells you about a problem, offer to help come up with a solution together. If your son is worried about an upcoming math test, for example, offering to help him study will lessen his concern about it.

Best Parenting Style Today To Keep Your Family Together

In most situations, resist the urge to jump in and fix a problem for your child — instead, think it through and come up with possible solutions together. Problem-solve *with* kids, rather than *for* them. By taking an active role, kids learn how to tackle a problem independently.

Keep things in perspective. Kids sometimes worry about things that have already happened. That's where parents can offer some big-picture perspective. Maybe your daughter got a really bad haircut that sent her home in tears. Let her know you understand how upset she feels, then remind her that her hair will grow and help her come up with a cool new way to style it in the meantime. If your son is worried about whether he'll get the lead in the school play, remind him that there's a play every season — if he doesn't get the part he wants this time, he'll have other opportunities. Acknowledge how important this is to him and let him know that — regardless of the outcome — you're proud that he tried out and gave it his best shot.

Without minimizing a child's feelings, point out that many problems are temporary and solvable, and that there will be better days and other opportunities to try again. Teaching kids to keep problems in perspective can lessen their worry and help build strength, resilience, and the optimism to try again. Remind your kids that whatever happens, things will be OK.

Make a difference. Sometimes kids worry about big stuff — like terrorism, war, or global warming — that they hear about at school or on the news. Parents can help by discussing these issues, offering accurate information, and correcting any misconceptions kids might have. Try to reassure kids by talking about what adults are doing to tackle the problem to keep them safe.

Be aware that your own reaction to global events affects kids, too. If you express anger and stress about a world event that's beyond your control, kids are likely to react that way too. But if you express your concern by taking a proactive approach to make a positive difference, your kids will feel more optimistic and empowered to do the same. So look for

Best Parenting Style Today To Keep Your Family Together

things you can do with your kids to help all of you feel like you're making a positive difference. You may not be able to go stop a war, for example, but your family can contribute to an organization that works for peace or helps kids in war-torn countries. Or your family might perform community service to give your kids the experience of volunteering.

Offer reassurance and comfort. Sometimes when kids are worried, what they need most is a parent's reassurance and comfort. It might come in the form of a hug, some heartfelt words, or time spent together. It helps kids to know that, whatever happens, parents will be there with love and support.

Sometimes kids need parents to show them how to let go of worry rather than dwell on it. Know when it's time to move on, and help kids shift gears. Lead the way by introducing a topic that's more upbeat or an activity that will create a lighter mood.

Be a good role model. The most powerful lessons we teach kids are the ones we demonstrate. Your response to your own worries can go a long way toward teaching your kids how to deal with everyday challenges. If you're rattled or angry when dealing with a to-do list that's too long, your child will learn that as the appropriate response to stress.

Instead, look on the bright side and voice optimistic thoughts about your own situations at least as frequently as you talk about what worries you. Set a good example with your reactions to problems and setbacks. Responding with optimism and confidence teaches kids that problems are temporary and tomorrow's another day. Bouncing back with a can-do attitude will help your kids do the same.

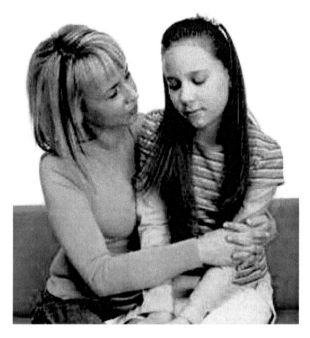

Best Parenting Style Today To Keep Your Family Together

Chapter 10

Helping Your Child Through a Divorce

Divorce is stressful for parents and kids alike. Although reactions will depend on a child's age, temperament, and the circumstances surrounding the split, many kids feel sad, frustrated, angry, and anxious — and it's not uncommon for them to act out because of those feelings.

Fortunately, parents can help their kids during a divorce. By minimizing the tension the situation creates, being patient as everyone adjusts to the new situation, and responding openly and honestly to your kids' concerns, you can help them through this difficult time.

Crucial to a child's ability to get through a divorce is the ability of the divorcing parents to maintain a civil relationship. Conflict between parents — whether they're separated, divorced, or still together — causes major stress for kids that can last well beyond childhood.

Best Parenting Style Today To Keep Your Family Together

Telling Kids About Divorce

As soon as you're certain of your plans, talk to your child about your decision to live apart. Although there's no easy way to break the news, if possible have both parents be there for this conversation. And it's important to leave feelings of anger, guilt, or blame out of it.

Although the discussion about divorce should be tailored to a child's age, maturity, and temperament, be sure to convey one basic message: What happened is between mom and dad and does not have anything to do with the kids. Most kids will feel they are to blame even after parents have said that they are not. So it's vital for parents to keep providing this reassurance.

Give kids enough information to prepare them for any upcoming changes in their lives. Try to answer their questions as truthfully as possible, in a way that they can understand and process. Remember that kids don't need to know every last detail — they just need to know enough to understand clearly how their lives are going to change.

With younger kids, it's best to keep it simple. You might say something like: "Mom and dad are going to live in different houses so they don't fight so much, but we both love you very much and will try to help you get through this."

Best Parenting Style Today To Keep Your Family Together

Older kids and teens may be more in tune with what parents have been going through, and may have more probing — and difficult — questions about things based on what they've overheard and picked up on from conversations and fights.

Tell kids who are upset about the news that you recognize and care about their feelings and reassure them that all of their upset feelings are perfectly OK and understandable. You might say: "I know this is very upsetting for you. Can we try to think of something that would make you feel better?" or "We both love you and are sorry that mommy and daddy have to live apart."

Not all kids react right away. Let yours know that's OK too, and there will be other times to talk, if they want to. Some kids try to please their parents by acting as if everything is fine, or try to avoid any difficult feelings by denying that they feel any anger or sadness at the news.

Whatever your child's immediate reaction, it's important to provide answers and reassurance about how life will change and what will stay the same. Be ready with answers to these questions, even before they're asked:

- Who will I live with? Where will I go to school?
- Will I move?
- Where will mom live and where will dad live?
- Will I still get to see my friends?
- Will I have to go to a different school?
- Can I still go to camp this summer?
- Can I still do my favorite activities?

Try to be honest when addressing your child's concerns and provide reassurance that the family will get through this, even though it may take some time.

Helping Kids Cope

Divorce brings numerous changes and a very real sense of loss. Many kids — and parents — grieve the loss of the kind of family they had hoped for, and children especially miss the presence of a parent and the family life they had. That's why it's common and very natural for some kids to hold out hope that their parents will someday get back together — even after the finality of divorce has been explained to them. Mourning the loss of a family is normal, but over time both you and your child will come to accept the new situation. So reassure kids that it's OK for them to wish that mom and dad will reunite, but also explain the finality of your decisions.

Here are some ways to help kids cope with the upset of a divorce:

- **Encourage honesty.** Kids need to know that their feelings are important to their parents and that they'll be taken seriously.

- **Help them put their feelings into words.** Children's behavior can often clue you in to their feelings of sadness or anger. Let them voice their emotions and help them to label them, without trying to change their emotions or explain them away. You might say: "It seems as if you're feeling sad right now. Do you know what's making you feel so sad?" Be a good listener when they respond, even if it's difficult for you to hear what they have to say.

Best Parenting Style Today To Keep Your Family Together

- **Legitimize their feelings.** Saying "I know you feel sad now" or "I know it feels lonely without dad here" lets kids know that their feelings are valid. It's important to encourage kids to get it all out before you start offering ways to make it better.

- **Offer support.** Ask, "What do you think will help you feel better?" They might not be able to name something, but you can suggest a few ideas — maybe just to sit together for a while, take a walk, or hold a favorite stuffed animal. Younger kids might especially appreciate an offer to call daddy on the phone or to make a picture to give to mommy when she comes at the end of the day.

- **Keep yourself healthy.** For many adults, separation and divorce is one of the most stressful life events they ever go through. That pressure may be amplified by custody and financial issues, which can bring out the worst in people. Finding ways to manage your own stress is essential for you and your entire family. Keeping yourself as physically and emotionally healthy as possible can help combat the effects of stress, and by making sure you're taking care of your own needs, you can ensure that you'll be in the best possible shape to take care of your family.

- **Keep the details in check.** Take care to ensure privacy when discussing the details of the divorce with friends, family, or your lawyer. Try to keep your interactions with your ex as civil as possible, especially when you're interacting in front of the kids. Take the high road — don't resort to blaming or name-calling within earshot of your children, no matter what the circumstances of the separation. This is especially important in an "at fault" divorce where there have been especially hurtful events, like infidelity.

- **Get help.** This is not the time to go it alone. Find a support group, talk to others who have gone through this, use online resources, or ask your doctor or religious leaders to refer you to other resources. Getting help yourself sets a good example for your kids on how to make a healthy adjustment to this major change. Help from a counselor, therapist, or friend will also maintain healthy boundaries with your kids. It's very important not to lean on your kids for support. Older kids and those who are eager to please may try to make you feel better by offering a shoulder to cry on. No matter how tempting that is, it's best not to let them be the provider of your emotional support. Let your kids know how touched you are by their caring nature and kindness, but do your venting to a friend or therapist.

Consistency and routine can go a long way toward providing comfort and familiarity that can help your family during this major life change. When possible, minimize unpredictable schedules, transitions, or abrupt separations.

Especially during a divorce, kids will benefit from one-on-one time with each parent. No matter how inconvenient, try to accommodate your ex-partner as you figure out visitation schedules.

It's natural that you'll be concerned about how a child is coping with this change. The best thing that you can do is trust your instincts and rely on what you know about your kids. Does they seem to be acting differently than usual? Is a child doing things like regressing to younger behaviors,

Best Parenting Style Today To Keep Your Family Together

such as thumb-sucking or bedwetting? Do emotions seem to be getting in the way of everyday routines, like school and social life?

Depression, moodiness, acting out, poor performance in school, use of alcohol or other drugs, sexual activity, or chronic oppositional behavior can all signal that kids are having trouble. Teens may have behavior problems, exhibit depression, show poor school performance, run away from home, or get into trouble with the law. Regardless of whether such troubles are related to the divorce, they are serious problems that affect a teen's well-being and indicate the need for outside help.

Fighting in Front of the Kids

Although the occasional argument between parents is expected even in a healthy family, living in a battleground of continual hostility and unresolved conflict can place a heavy burden on any child. Screaming, fighting, arguing, or violence can make kids fearful and apprehensive.

Witnessing parental conflict presents an inappropriate model for kids, who are still learning how to deal with their own relationships. Kids whose parents maintain anger and hostility are much more likely to have continued emotional and behavioral difficulties that last beyond childhood.

Talking with a mediator or divorce counselor can help couples air their grievances and hurt to each other in a way that doesn't cause harm to the children. Though it may be difficult, working together in this way will spare kids the hurt caused by continued bitterness and anger.

Adjusting to a New Living Situation

Because divorce can be such a big change, adjustments in living arrangements should be handled gradually.

Several types of living situations should be considered:

- one parent may have custody
- joint custody in which both parents share in the legal decisions about the child, but the child lives primarily with one parent and visits the other

- shared joint custody in which decisions are shared and so is physical custody

There's no simple solution to this. Although some kids can thrive spending half their time with each parent, others seem to need the stability of having one "home" and visiting with the other parent. Some parents choose to both remain in the same home — but this only works in the rarest of circumstances and in general should be avoided.

Whatever arrangement you choose, your child's needs should always come first. Avoid getting involved in a tug of war as a way to "win." When deciding how to handle holidays, birthdays, and vacations, stay focused on what's best for the kids. It's important for parents to resolve these issues themselves and not ask the kids to choose.

During the preteen years, when kids become more involved with activities apart from their parents, they may need different schedules to accommodate their changing priorities. Ideally, kids benefit most from consistent support from both parents, but they may resist equal time-sharing if it interrupts school or their social lives. Be prepared for their thoughts on time-sharing, and try to be flexible.

Your child may refuse to share time with you and your spouse equally and may try to take sides. If this occurs, as hard as it is, try not to take it personally. Maintain the visitation schedule and emphasize the importance of the involvement of both parents.

Kids sometimes propose spending an entire summer, semester, or school year with the noncustodial parent. But this may not reflect that they want to move. Listen to and explore these options if they're brought up.

Parenting Under Pressure

It's hard to maintain your role as a parent when going through any kind of emotional turmoil. You might be tempted to depend on kids for emotional support or to ask them to report back on what the other parent is doing. Resist such urges — mothers and fathers should work hard to keep their parental roles in place. Kids, no matter how much they try to understand what you're going through, are still just kids.

Consistency in routine and discipline across the households is important. Similar expectations regarding bedtimes, rules, and homework will reduce anxiety. Wherever possible work with the other parent to maintain consistent rules — and even when you can't enforce them in your ex-partner's home, you can stick to them in yours.

It's important to maintain as much normalcy as possible after a divorce by keeping regular routines, including mealtimes, house rules about behavior, and discipline. Relaxing limits, especially during a time of change, tends to make kids insecure and reduces your chances of regaining appropriate parental authority later.

Resist the urge to drop routines and spoil kids upset about a divorce by letting them break rules or not enforcing limits. You should feel free to lavish affection on them — kids don't get spoiled by too many hugs or comforting words — but buying things to replace love or allowing kids to act any way they want is not in their best interests and you may have a hard time trying to reign them back in once the dust settles.

Divorce is a major crisis for a family. But if you and your former spouse can work together and maintain a civil relationship for the benefit of your children, the original family unit can continue to be a source of strength, even if stepfamilies enter the picture.

So remember to:

- **Get help dealing with your own painful feelings about the divorce.** If you're able to adjust, your kids will be more likely to do so, too. Also, getting needed emotional support and being able to air your feelings and thoughts with an adult will lessen the possibility of your child shouldering the unfair burden of your emotional concerns. Confidants may include trusted friends or family members or a therapist.

- **Be patient with yourself and with your child.** Emotional concerns, loss, and hurt following divorce take time to heal and this often happens in phases. That's healthy.

- **Recognize the signs of stress.** Consult your child's teacher, doctor, or a child therapist for guidance on how to handle specific problems you're concerned about.

Many of the elements that help kids in intact families thrive and be emotionally healthy are the same ones that help those from divorced families thrive and be emotionally healthy. With good support, kids can and do successfully make this life adjustment.

Best Parenting Style Today To Keep Your Family Together

Chapter 11

Questions and Answers About Sex

Answering kids' questions about sex is one of the responsibilities many parents dread most. Otherwise confident parents often feel tongue-tied and awkward when it comes to sex. But the subject shouldn't be avoided. By answering kids' questions as they arise, parents can help foster healthy feelings about sex.

When do kids start becoming curious about sex?

Children are human beings and therefore sexual beings. It's hard for parents to acknowledge this, just as it's hard for kids to think of their parents as sexually active. But even infants have curiosity about their own bodies, which is healthy and normal.

What sort of "sexual" behavior do young kids exhibit?

Toddlers will often touch themselves when they are naked, such as in the bathtub or while being diapered. At this stage of development, they have no modesty. Their parents' reaction will tell them whether their actions are acceptable. Toddlers should not be scolded or made to feel ashamed of being interested in their bodies. It is natural for children to be interested in their own bodies. Some parents may choose to casually ignore self-touching. Others may want to acknowledge that, while they know it feels good, it is a private matter. Parents can make it clear that they expect the child to keep that activity private.

Parents should only be concerned about masturbation if a child seems preoccupied with it to the exclusion of other activities. Victims of sexual abuse sometimes become preoccupied with self-stimulation.

Is it OK to use nicknames for private parts?

By the time a child is 3 years of age, parents may choose to use the correct anatomical words. They may sound clinical, but there is no reason why the proper label shouldn't be used when the child is capable of saying it. These words — penis, vagina, etc. — should be stated matter-of-factly, with no implied silliness. That way, the child learns to use them in a direct manner, without embarrassment.

In fact, this is what most parents do. A Gallup Poll showed that 67% of parents use actual names to refer to male and female body parts.

What do you tell a very young child who asks where babies come from?

Depending on the child's age, you can say that the baby grows from an egg in the mommy's womb, pointing to your stomach, and comes out of a special place, called the vagina. There is no need to explain the act of lovemaking because very young kids will not understand the concept.
However, you can say that when a man and a woman love each other, they like to be close to one another. Tell them that the man's sperm joins the woman's egg and then the baby begins to grow. Most kids under the age of 6 will accept this answer. Age-appropriate books on the subject are also helpful. Answer the question in a straightforward manner, and you will probably find that your child is satisfied with a little information at a time.

What should you do if you catch kids "playing doctor" (i.e., showing private parts to each other)?

Kids 3 to 6 years old are most likely to "play doctor." Many parents overreact when they witness or hear of such behavior. Heavy-handed scolding is **not** the way to deal with it. Nor should parents feel this is or will lead to promiscuous behavior. Often, the presence of a parent is enough to interrupt the play.

You may wish to direct your child's attention to another activity without making a lot of fuss. Later, sit down with your child for a talk. Explain that although you understand the interest in his or her friend's body, but that people are generally expected to keep their bodies covered in public. This way you have set limits without having made the child feel guilty.
This is also an appropriate age to begin to talk about good and bad touch. Tell kids that their bodies are their own and that they have the right to privacy. No one should touch kids if they don't like it or want it. Tell them that if anyone ever touches them in a way that feels strange or bad, they should tell that person to stop it and then tell you about it. Explain

that you want to know about anything that makes your kids feel bad or uncomfortable.

When should parents sit kids down for that all-important "birds and bees" talk?

Actually, never! Learning about sex should not occur in one all-or-nothing session. It should be more of an unfolding process, one in which kids learn, over time, what they need to know. Questions should be answered as they arise so that kids' natural curiosity is satisfied as they mature.

If your child doesn't ask questions about sex, don't just ignore the subject. At about age 5, you can begin to introduce books that approach sexuality on a developmentally appropriate level. Parents often have trouble finding the right words, but many excellent books are available to help.

At what age should nudity in the home be curtailed?

Families set their own standards for nudity, modesty, and privacy. Although every family's values are different, privacy is an important concept for all kids to learn. Parents should explain limits regarding privacy the same way that other house rules are explained — matter-of-factly — so that kids don't come to associate privacy with guilt or secrecy. Generally, they'll learn from the limits you establish for them.

To what extent can parents depend on schools to teach sex education?

Parents should begin the sex education process long before it starts in school. The introduction of formal sex education in the classroom varies; many schools start it in the fifth or sixth grade. Some of the topics addressed in sex-ed class may include anatomy, contraception, sexually transmitted diseases, and pregnancy. Parents should be open to continuing the dialogue and answering questions at home. Schools tend to teach mechanics and science more than values. This is an area where parents can and should have something to teach.

At what age should girls be told about menstruation?

Girls (and boys!) should have information about menstruation by about age 8, some of which may be provided in school. Instructional books are helpful, but moms should also share their own personal experiences with their daughters, including when their periods first started and what it felt like, and how, like many things, it wasn't such a big deal after a while.

Best Parenting Style Today To Keep Your Family Together

Chapter 12

Tips for Divorcing Parents

No guide can guarantee a way to steer kids unscathed through a divorce. Every situation — and every family — is different. But some commonsense guidelines might make the adjustment a bit easier.

These suggestions can make the process less painful for kids. Parents will need to interpret them in their own ways; honesty, sensitivity, self-control, and time itself will help the healing process. Be patient — not everyone's timetable is the same.

Encourage kids to openly discuss their feelings — positive or negative — about what's happening.

It's important for divorcing — and already divorced — parents to sit down with their kids and encourage them to say what they're thinking and feeling. But you'll need to keep this separate from your own feelings. Most often, children experience a sense of loss of family and may blame you or the other parent — or both — for what they perceive as a betrayal. So, you'll really need to be prepared to answer questions your kids might raise or to address their concerns.

Make talking about the divorce and how it's affecting your kids an ongoing process. As kids get older and become more mature, they might have questions or concerns that they hadn't thought of earlier. Even if it seems like you've gone over the same topics before, keep the dialogue open.

If you feel like you get too upset to be of real help to your kids, ask someone else (a relative, maybe) to talk to them. Group programs for kids of divorce run by schools or faith-based organizations are an excellent resource for kids going through this.

It's natural for kids to have many emotions about a divorce. They might feel guilty and imagine that they "caused" the problem. This is particularly true if they ever heard their parents argue about them. Kids may feel angry or frightened, or worried that they will be abandoned by or "divorced from" their parents.

Although kids may struggle with a divorce for quite some time, the real impact is usually felt over about a 2- to 3-year period. During this time, some will be able to voice their feelings but, depending on their age and development, other kids just won't have the words. They may instead act out or be depressed. For school-age kids, this is usually evident when their grades drop or they lose interest in activities. For younger children, these feelings are often expressed during play, too.

It may be tempting to tell a child not to feel a certain way, but kids (and adults, for that matter) have a right to their feelings. And if you try to force a "happy face," your kids may be less likely to share their true feelings with you.

Best Parenting Style Today To Keep Your Family Together

Don't bad-mouth your ex in front of the kids, even if you're still angry or feuding.

This is one of the hardest things to do. But it's important not to say bad things about your ex. Doing so often backfires and kids get angry at the parent who is saying the bad things. No child likes to hear a parent criticized, even if it is by the other parent. It's equally important to acknowledge real events. If, for example, one spouse has simply abandoned the family by moving out, you need to acknowledge what has happened. It isn't your responsibility to explain the ex-spouse's behavior — let him or her do so with the kids.

Try not to use kids as messengers or go-betweens, especially when you're feuding.

Kids don't need to feel that they must act as messengers between hostile parents or carry one adult's secrets or accusations about another. Don't question your child about what is happening in the other household — kids resent it when they feel that they're being asked to "spy" on the other parent. Wherever possible, communicate directly with the other parent about relevant matters, such as scheduling, visitation, health issues, or school problems.

Expect resistance and difficulties as kids adjust to a new mate or the mate's kids.

New relationships, blended families, and remarriages are among the most difficult aspects of the divorce process. A new, blended family doesn't eliminate the impact of divorce — in fact, research shows that kids in these new families experience problems similar to those who remain with a single parent.

So, it's important to assure kids that they still have a mother and father who care for them and to help them blend into a new family structure. Don't expect kids to accept a stepparent as another parent right away, though — that will take time. The initial role of a stepparent is that of another caring adult in a child's life. Tell kids that the stepparent needs to be respected the same way that they respect teachers, coaches, and other adults who help them.

Seek support groups, friendships, and counseling. Single parents need all the help they can get.

Support from clergy, friends, relatives, and groups such as Parents Without Partners can help parents and their kids adjust to separation and divorce. Kids can meet others who've developed successful relationships with separated parents and can confide in each other, while adults need special support through these trying times.

Whenever possible, kids should be encouraged to have as positive an outlook on both parents as they can. Even under the best of circumstances, separation and divorce can be painful and disappointing for many kids.

And, of course, it's emotionally difficult for the parents. So it's understandable that, despite their best intentions, some parents might broadcast their pain and anger. But parents who can foster a positive adjustment and good times, even during difficult circumstances, will go a long way toward helping their kids — and themselves — adapt and move on.

Best Parenting Style Today To Keep Your Family Together

Best Parenting Style Today To Keep Your Family Together

What You Need to Know About Drugs: Cocaine and Crack

What It Is:

Cocaine is a white powder that comes from the dried leaves of the coca plant. Crack cocaine is a form of the drug that gives a very quick, intense high.

Crack is made by cooking cocaine powder with baking soda, then breaking it into small pieces called rocks. It got its name because it crackles when it is heated and smoked.

Crack cocaine looks like white or tan pellets (sort of like gerbil or dry cat food). Both cocaine and crack are very addictive — and extremely dangerous.

Sometimes Called:

coke, rock, snow, blow, white, toot, nose candy, base, flake, powder, basa, smack

How It's Used:

Cocaine is inhaled or snorted through the nose or injected into a vein. Crack is smoked in a pipe.

What It Does:

Cocaine is a stimulant, which means that it produces a fast, intense feeling of power and energy. Then it wears off (crack wears off very quickly) and the user feels depressed and nervous and craves more of the drug to feel good again.

Cocaine is so addictive that someone can get hooked after trying it just once.

Snorting cocaine can damage the septum between the nostrils, causing a hole in the middle of the nose.

Cocaine makes the heart beat faster, and blood pressure and body temperature rise. It can make a person's heart beat abnormally. Cocaine is so dangerous that using it just once can cause a heart attack or stroke that can be fatal.

Chapter 13

How Can Spirituality Affect Your Family's Health?

Can spirituality promote a healthier physical life for your family? Recent medical studies indicate that spiritual people exhibit fewer self-destructive behaviors (suicide, smoking, and drug and alcohol abuse, for example), less stress, and a greater total life satisfaction.

Much of the research linking spiritual and physical health has involved elderly patients; however, the data offer a glimpse into a possible tie between a spiritual life and good health for people of all ages.

Although spirituality has been shown to reduce depression, improve blood pressure, and boost the immune system, religious beliefs should **not** interfere with the medical care kids receive.

So what exactly is spirituality and how can it enhance your family's health?

Best Parenting Style Today To Keep Your Family Together

Spirituality and Physical Health

Doctors and scientists once avoided the study of spirituality in connection to medicine, but findings within the past 10 years have made some take a second look. Studies show that religion and faith can help to promote good health and fight disease by:

- offering additional social supports, such as religious outreach groups
- improving coping skills through prayer and a philosophy that all things have a purpose

Although research on kids hasn't been done, many studies focusing on adults point to the positive effects of spirituality on medical outcome:

- In a 7-year study of senior citizens, religious involvement was associated with less physical disability and less depression. Death rates were lower than expected before an important religious holiday, which suggested to researchers that faith might have postponed death in these cases.

- Elderly people who regularly attended religious services had healthier immune systems than those who didn't. They were also more likely to have consistently lower blood pressure.

-
- Patients undergoing open-heart surgery who received strength and comfort from their religion were three times more likely to survive than those who had no religious ties.

Spirituality and Mental Health

Religious and spiritual beliefs are an important part of how many people deal with life's joys and hardships. Faith can provide people with a sense of purpose and guidelines for living.

When families face tough situations, including health problems, their religious beliefs and practices can help them fight feelings of helplessness, restore meaning and order to life situations, and promote regaining a sense of control. For some families, spirituality can be a powerful and important source of strength.

Medical studies have confirmed that spirituality can have a profound effect on mental states. In a study of men who were hospitalized, nearly half rated religion as helpful in coping with their illness. A second study showed that the more religious patients were, the more quickly they recovered from some disorders. A third study revealed that high levels of hope and optimism, key factors in fighting depression, were found among those who strictly practiced their religion.

Best Parenting Style Today To Keep Your Family Together

Can Spiritual Beliefs Enhance Parenting?

Attending organized religious services may help some families connect with their spiritual values, but it's not the only way. Less traditional paths also can help kids and parents find spiritual meaning.

To foster spirituality within your own family, you may want to examine your own values. Ask yourself: What is important to me? How well do my daily activities mirror my values? Do I neglect issues that matter to me because I'm busy spending time on things that matter less?
Here are other suggestions to start your family's spiritual journey:

- Explore your roots. In examining your shared past, you and your kids may connect with values of earlier times and places, and gain a sense of your extended family's history and values.

- Examine your involvement in the community. If you're already involved in a group, maybe you will want to take on a larger role — first for you, then as a role model for your kids. If you haven't joined a community group, consider investigating those in your area.

- Recall the feelings you had at the birth or adoption of your child. Try to get back to that moment in your mind, remembering the hopes and dreams you had. It can be the start of a search for similar or related feelings in your everyday life.

- Share some silence with your kids. Take a few minutes for silent meditation alone or together. Think about parenthood, your life as an individual, and your place in the larger scheme of things. Spend time discussing these thoughts with your kids and listen to their ideas on what spirituality means.

- Take a nature walk. Nature has long been an inspiration and spiritual guide. A walk will relax you and allow you to contemplate the wonders of the world around you.

- Read books that express spiritual ideas with your kids and share your thoughts about what you're reading.

This search can be conducted on your own or as part of a larger group — a religious community, friends, or your own family. Making a spiritual journey might help you and your family live a healthier life, both emotionally and physically.

Reviewed by: Steven Dowshen, MD

Chapter 14

5 Secrets for Handling Difficult Teen Parenting Situations

Move from conflict to cooperation with these 5 Secrets.

The most common issues between parents and teens arise due to poor communication, power struggles and a lack of empathy. If you use the same parenting methods that you did when your teen was a child, you won't get positive results. You'll just exhaust your energy.

There are five secrets to help you move from conflict to cooperation. Let the acronym - CLEAR - aid you in remembering what they are.

Difficult Teens:
Suggestions for Parents

Best Parenting Style Today To Keep Your Family Together

1. Connect

Connection is everything. You do that by having rapport. It's easy to be in rapport when you like your teen. Yet teenagers are often difficult to like. Did you know that liking someone is not a prerequisite for rapport? The ability to find something likable, however, is necessary.

To develop rapport, focus on something you can appreciate about your son or daughter. It can be a physical trait (eye color or bright smile), character trait or talent you can admire. If that feels hard, think back to when your child was an infant or toddler. Focusing on a positive aspect of your teen will build connection and prepare you for your next interaction. Then, notice the difference as you feel more connected and in accord with each other.

2. Listen

Before you can be a good listener, you need to be willing to get more information. When you listen without being attached to your own point of view, you can become open and less defensive. I suggest you listen consciously without interrupting. Imagine you are hearing the words from the smartest and most admirable person you know.

Identify feelings, resist the impulse to dismiss feelings or give unsolicited advice. Be interested in your teen; don't make the conversation about you. That would be a turn-off, and over time, you would run the risk of turning your teenager further away, eventually looking for family and "love" in all the wrong places.

3. Empathy

Many arguments and much strife would be avoided if you take a moment to step into teens' shoes, to learn how they perceive their situation. Then, empathize right away. This ability to truly hear and seek to understand causes your teen to feel heard--vital for smooth communications.

When you empathize, be sincere. Focus on the words and feelings that are given and speak to them. Let your teen know you feel their pain or their joy. Experiencing empathy feels like receiving a hug. Without it, we feel empty and alone. Empathy enhances self-worth and builds harmonious and trustful relationships.

4. Acknowledge

Acknowledge your teen's thoughts, feelings, or complaints; this does NOT mean that you are agreeing with them! You are simply and effectively connecting to them by validating what you heard. Some of you might be tempted to skip this step, so strong is our "need to be right." Don't do it!

Kids need to feel heard so that they know it's safe to talk to you. Empathy together with acknowledgement magically combines into a healing balm for the child in the "pain of anger." Even out-of-control kids will begin to let go of their resistance.

5. Request

In coaching teens to success, there is an emphasis on making requests vs. demands. A request is asking someone to do something. When you demand, you paint yourself into a corner. If a demand is declined, it can cause damage to the relationship. Why? Because the biggest stumbling block you'll run into relates to being controlling. Control leads to resentment and resistance - not cooperation.

Here's an example of a request that states your clear expectation, "I request that you don't call your sister names or use put-downs. If you have suggestions that you think would be helpful to her, and then say it in a respectful and constructive way." Teens are more likely to listen when you make a respectful request.

If you find that you resort to demanding things, you're probably letting your frustrations build up and are waiting too long to ask for what you want.

teens

We're
Waiting
because
Our Dream
Won't

Best Parenting Style Today To Keep Your Family Together

Ten tips for one of the toughest jobs on earth!

Read books about puberty. Think back on your own. Remember your struggles with acne, your embarrassment at developing early - or late. Expect some mood changes in your typically sunny child, and be prepared for more conflict as she finds her way as an individual. Parents who know what's coming can cope with it better. And the more you know, the better you can prepare your child.

Talk to Your Child Early Enough

Talking about menstruation or wet dreams after they've already started means you are too late. Answer the early questions kids have about their bodies, the differences between boys and girls, and where babies come from. Don't overload them with information - just answer their questions. You know your child. You can hear when he's starting to tell jokes about sex, or when his attention to his own appearance is increasing. This is a good time to jump in with your own questions: "Are you noticing any changes in your body? Are you having any strange feelings? Are you sad sometimes and don't know why?" A yearly physical exam is a great time to bring up these things. A doctor can tell a pre-adolescent child and her parents what to expect in the next few years. The exam can serve as a jumping-off point for a good parent/child discussion of puberty. The later you wait to have this discussion, the more likely your child will be to form misconceptions or become embarrassed about or afraid of his physical and emotional changes. Furthermore, the earlier you open the lines of communication on these subjects, the better chance you have of keeping them open through puberty. Give your child books on puberty written for kids going through it. Encourage them to access the KidsHealth article on puberty written for kids. Share memories of your own adolescence with your child. There's nothing like knowing that Mom or Dad went through it, too, to put a child more at ease.

Encourage the Group Connection

Your student's friends are her greatest source of comfort and safety during the school day. Do what you can to help her stay connected. If the rest are walking, let yours walk too. If you're driving, then pick up some others. Try not to isolate your kid from the group. The move to secondary school shakes some long established groups. Keep an eye on it. Check out any new members. Be wary if your students' group breaks up. Do what you can to help establish new connections. Loners are vulnerable and without support in a new and scary environment.

Best Parenting Style Today To Keep Your Family Together

Get Connected Stay Connected

Information is your best tool in helping your child be successful. Go to the parent evenings. Introduce yourself to teachers. Introduce yourself to consellors. If your student has a special ed. background, be in touch with the special ed. department. Knowing someone at home cares gives a boost to your child's profile in most classes. Many schools publish student agenda books with pages on expectations and routines. Ask to see it and read it. Many schools publish student agenda books with pages on expectations and routines. Ask to see it and read it. Most schools publish dates for newsletters, interim reports and major reports to parents. Post the list. Ask for the newsletters. Ask for the report cards. Talk about the report cards. Go to the parent teacher interviews; trouble or not. Let your student know it's important " walk your talk. Let the teachers know it's important " walk your talk. Do you have the school web site bookmarked? Do any of the teachers have a course website?

Be Alert Be Responsive

A lot of kids are poor self-reporters. They minimize troubles, are slow to ask for help, are afraid to rock the boat, and don't like to upset you. Trust your instinct. You know your kid best. Make the call if you suspect something's wrong. Don't wait for the report card. Make sure your telephone info is up to date on school records. Have you given the school YOUR E mail address? Know the reasons for poorer than expected grades. Know what the solutions are and support them. Get the full story on any incidents. Talk to both sides. Not satisfied? Get help. Call a counsellor. Call a Vice Principal. Call a principal.

Most kids will be just fine. There are things you can do to make it easier, on them and ultimately, on you. A good start is very important. A bad start can take a long time to fix.

Chapter 15

Make Time -- Don't Mark Time with your young adolescent

Is your family time-starved? Are you always trying to get things done when the reality is that one is never done? Over and over again, young adolescents say that what they would really like is more time with their parents, not more things in their lives. Here are several easy-to-implement tips that will give you more time to spend with your young adolescent.

1. **Less is more.** Do less. On the weekends don't make each day a 24 hour marathon. Plan to accomplish one thing - do the laundry, buy the groceries or clean the apartment - and plan on some time for the entire family to do something together.

2. **Don't divide to conquer.** While it may be more efficient for dad to go to the grocery store while mom washes the car, and the kids

do homework, that means that no one is working together. If Suzy goes to the store with her parent, she will not only be helping and making a contribution to the family, but will miss out on an opportunity to spend essential time with that parent.

3. **NO, NO, NO.** Say yes only to those requests that you genuinely want to do. Remember that your young adolescent is wathing you to see how you respond to multiple requests and allocate your time. Ask yourself, "If I get involved in this project, how will it impact my family?"

4. **Yes, Yes, Yes.** Say yes to those activities that model the kind of involvement you want your young adolescent to emulate, and get them involved as well. Turn off the TV on weekends so you can just sit around and play a game and talk.

Contributed courtesy of the National Middle School Association

Best Parenting Style Today To Keep Your Family Together

Best Parenting Style Today To Keep Your Family Together

6 Tips for Successful and Effective Parenting

Need help to a more effective parenting? Here are some tips that you may find them useful. While they are not exhaustive but it should provide a background to expand your parenting skills.

1. Unconditional Love

All children must be aware of their parent's unconditional love for them. *ie. We must continue to love our child regardless of their success or failure.* A child that knows they are loved and feels that love on a daily basis is more likely to be successful in school and grow up to be a loving, concerned parent themselves.

2. Communication is Key

An open line of communication is perhaps one of the most important aspects of parenting. Many children feel that parents or adults in general, don't listen to them long enough to hear what they're actually saying.

Instead of saying ―How dare you stay out past your curfew?" try something such as ―I worry when you're late, thinking that something is wrong. What can we do to make sure this doesn't happen again?"

3. Be Fair and Honest

All children learn by example. Leading by example is a great way to instill a healthy set of values in your child. All parents hopefully tell their children that lying is not acceptable. It's important to live your life as a positive example for your child, remembering that kids often see and hear much more than we realize.

Allowing your child to hear you telling ―little white lies" or watching you keep the extra money the clerk gave by mistake, or seeing you somehow shirking your duties and responsibilities as an adult are all ways of encouraging dishonesty and negative behavior.

Best Parenting Style Today To Keep Your Family Together

4. Encourage Success

Encourage your child to succeed in whatever venture they decide to undertake. Whether it's getting good grades, excelling at sports, or being involved with other productive activities, be sure to offer plenty of praise, understanding, and patience. Also, parents should make it their purpose to be supportive in whatever endeavor their child decides upon. This is not to say that a parent's opinion and advice aren't needed or warranted, however, the manner in which we express those thoughts and feelings really do make an inherit difference.

5. Be Consistent

When disciplining your children, consistency is of the utmost importance. The moment a child realizes that you are merely making idle threats and not following through when it comes time to dole out discipline, they'll take advantage of this and never learn there are consequences for all of our actions.

Discipline should never depend upon the parent's mood or whether or not they had a bad day at the office. The same exact consequences must be used each and every time the unwanted behavior happens regardless of any outlying factors. Children need their world outlined in black and white, with boundaries, rules and supervision.

6. Be Positive

Although at one time or another it may seem that life is full of adversity and obstacles, it's important for those of us with children to remain as positive as possible. Realizing that a child is similar to tiny a sponge, soaking up all the information they can and absorbing everything around them, we must keep in mind that our actions and everything we say has a profound effect on our children.

Best Parenting Style Today To Keep Your Family Together

Core Parenting Tips

Some people go through life wondering how their lives would have been different if only their parents had done one thing or another. They wonder what could have been had their folks taken some parenting tips to heart. Yet when they become parents themselves, they end up repeating the very behavior they now lament. There is an exercise that parents can perform which will help them to break that cycle.

Ask yourself one question: What are one or two parenting tips that would make the biggest difference in your own child's life? Think about that for a moment. Take a few minutes free of distractions. Relax and really think about the question. What impact will that one tip have on the quality of your life, your child's life, and your relationship? Then write your parenting tips down. It is not enough to verbalize it in your head. You must write the parenting tips down on a piece of paper and read it to yourself. In most cases, what you wrote down will reveal to you the very essence of your own parenting beliefs.

When you write it down, it forces you to stick with what you came up with. If you are having difficulty with determining your core beliefs, visualize that your child has grown up with children of her own and has come to you for parenting advice.

After you have written it down, reflect upon your own childhood. How were you raised? How did your parents treat you? How did they respond to you when you needed them, physically and emotionally? How did your upbringing shape your feelings about yourself? In reflecting on your own upbringing, think about what their core belief was that guided their own parenting, as if you had gone to them and asked them that very question. Try to distill your parents' beliefs into one or two sentences and write that down below your own core belief. If mom and dad had different beliefs, write each one down.

Now see how your beliefs compare to theirs. How similar or different are they? What are your reactions to what you have written down?
Performing this exercise allows you to take a long, hard look at yourself and your upbringing. Once you can communicate this to yourself, you can make adjustments of your own.

Best Parenting Style Today To Keep Your Family Together

Effective Parenting Skills

As any parent will tell you, the one thing they most desire is to raise a happy, healthy, well-adjusted child who will become a contributing member of society. However, parenting is a full-time job with a lifelong commitment, one that must be continuously worked at to be improved upon.

Parents of any age with any number of children would benefit from making it a point to sharpen their parenting and communication skills. While there's no right or wrong way to be a parent, there are several ways to be the best parent possible, such as keeping your child safe, spending time with them, monitoring their activities, providing for their needs, and showing them love and affection.

Punishment vs. Discipline
While punishing your child may indeed cause improved behavior, it may also breed fear, anger and withdrawal. Punishment, whether in physical form or otherwise, is really about controlling a child rather than teaching them right from wrong. Discipline is about showing a child that they must expect consequences for their actions and that they are responsible for making the right choices in life. In short, as parents, we have to instill a sense of responsibility and accountability in our children.

Parenting and Your Child's School
Many schools are now taking the initiative to bridge the gap between parents and educators by implementing programs offering helpful parenting advice. By getting the parents actively involved in the learning process, children tend to show an increase in interest in their own education.

School-based workshops give families the information they need to develop effective parenting skills, as well as the opportunity to become an active member in their child's school. Informative newsletters and training programs covering everything from language development and learning skills to proper nutrition to anger management are all ways that schools and parents can work together to enhance education.

Best Parenting Style Today To Keep Your Family Together

Studies have shown a definitive decrease in school violence and a noticeable increase in student performance and participation in extracurricular activities when parents play an active role in their education. As supportive home environment is one of the best things you can do for your school-age child to ensure a successful transition into adulthood.

Best Parenting Style Today To Keep Your Family Together

Handling Parenting Advice

People are always willing to hand out parenting advice. Many times you do not even ask for it. Sometimes handling parenting advice can be difficult, but it is important to remember that most of the time people are only trying to help you out, not put down your way of parenting or your skills as a parent. You should simply learn the best ways to handle parenting advice.

Unsolicited Advice

The most common form of parenting advice is that which you do ask to get. People will sometimes feel the need to share their parenting tips with you and you really do not care to listen. However, for the sake of being nice and not being rude, you listen.

The best way to handle unsolicited parenting advice is just that – listen. You may actually be surprised from time to time and learn something you can actually use. Thank the person for sharing and move on from there.

If a person becomes quite annoying, though, you may have to say something. You can still be polite, though. You can simply say that you appreciate the fact they are trying to help, but you have your own methods and they are working out fine for you.

Friendly Advice

Friends are there for you through anything. That includes parenting where your friends are sure to want to share all the parenting advice they can with you. Your friends, though, know when you need it and when you don't. You will find that your friends may not just offer up advice, but rather wait for you to ask. Keep that in mind and when you want help from your friends – ask them for it.

Friendly advice is some of the best advice because they know you and your kids. They know if something might work for you or not and they usually are up front with things. They are often usually not pushy and don't care if you use their advice or not.

Professional Advice

Professional parenting advice is some of the best advice you can get. Professionals, like doctors or psychologists, know what they are talking about. Not only have they been educated on parenting, but they have also had plenty of experience with children. They can give you ideas and advice that work and that have been tried before. They can offer you an objective source of advice that you can trust.

Best Parenting Style Today To Keep Your Family Together

Chapter 16

Keys to Successful Single Parenting

Single parenting is something more and more parents are facing. There are many reasons why a parent may be facing single parenting, but all have the same basic struggles and issues.

Being a single parent means you are parenting a child by yourself with the other parent present all the time. In short, a single parent is someone who does not live with their child's father or mother. There can be many reasons for this. A parent could be divorced, widowed or not be with the child's other parent.

Single parenting can be difficult. It can be hard to handle a child all by yourself and at times it can be frustrating. It is often hard to juggle the responsibilities of parenting and all the other things you have to do. Without someone else there everything falls on your shoulders.

There are certain things that single parents can do to help make things easier on themselves and on their child. The following is a list of some things you can do to make being a single parent easier. Theses things can help you to keep order and sanity in your household.

Best Parenting Style Today To Keep Your Family Together

- Get organized. Organization is essential to a single parent. If you are not organized then you definitely will face plenty of frustration. Being organized means setting schedules, keeping your home organized and staying on top of everyday tasks.

-

- Know the roles. Many times in a single parent home the child ends up taking on more responsibility than they should have to. In order to keep the roles defined a parent has to be sure they are not expecting too much from their child. A child should be a child and not be expected to pick up the slack of the absent parent.

-

- Take a break. Every parent needs a break. When you have a partner there it can be easy to steal some alone time, but when you are doing it alone you have to make alone time. Find a babysitter or have family help out, by getting some time away from your child every now and then. You will both benefit from the break.

-

- Include your child. While you do not want to have your child pick up the role of the absent parent, involving them more and working as a team can be helpful. You can work together and as a team to get daily chores done. It can really strengthen your bond and make the child feel good about themselves when you treat them with respect and allow them to help out.

-

Single parenting is not always easy, but it is very rewarding. To raise a child by yourself is a great accomplishment. You will know that you are responsible for the wonderful person your child is and that you did it all by yourself. This is enough to make everyday easier to get through and make you glad you and your child have the special bond that can only come from single parenting.

Best Parenting Style Today To Keep Your Family Together

Best Parenting Style Today To Keep Your Family Together

Parenting Advice For Work At Home Moms

Most people know about all of the benefits of working from home and becoming self-employed. You get to work where you want to and when you want to. However, working from home for parents can be very difficult.

Work at home parents have to schedule their work around their family. It is hard to be productive with children constantly at your feet.

Working at home and trying to parent takes some skill and careful planning.

One of the most important skills to have when you are a parent working from home is time management. You need to be able to schedule your own hours and stick to them. Make the most of each working hour. It can

141 | P e a c e

help to make a to do list for work each day and plan a week or month ahead of time. Let your spouse in on your schedule, as well as your kids so they will know when you are working and when you are off the clock. Make the most of your time - whether you are working or not.

Working from home takes a lot of self-discipline. Many people do not take advantage of working from home either because they are scared or they simply can't work without someone else directing them on what needs to be done each day. Self-discipline is necessary to succeed in your work at home career. You need to be able to set your own hours and work when you are supposed to.

Another necessity in self-employment is perseverance. Learn from your mistakes without taking them personally. Move on and keep going no matter what. Even the most successful business owners have made mistakes, but they learned from them and moved on by not taking them to heart.

Lastly, you need a space that is comfortable for you to work in whether it is your own room or the kitchen table. Keeping this consistent will help your kids realize that when you are in that space you are working, and they should wait to speak to you unless it's an emergency.

Parenting Help for Manipulative Tantrums

At the joyous age of two through four, temper tantrums can creep in without warning. It is a frustrating event, and even the most prepared parent can't help but feel helpless at times. Fortunately, parenting help for tantrums isn't hard to find. There are some simple techniques you can perform for some parenting help during the most tempestuous of tantrums.

First, you should understand what kind of tantrum the child is having. The tantrum can be temperamental, manipulative, or verbal frustration. A manipulative tantrum, for example, is when the child has a tantrum because he or she did not get her own way. Without much parenting help, the manipulative tantrum will go away when ignored. You may wish to move the child into another room while the tantrum plays itself out, advising the child that when the tantrum is done, he or she may rejoin the rest of the family.

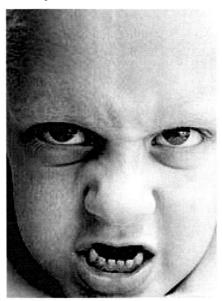

The child is not sophisticated enough to realize that they can throw a fit in order to get their own way. They just simply break down. However, if

Best Parenting Style Today To Keep Your Family Together

parenting help is ignored and mom gives in, the behavior will be reinforced and rewarded. The child will then realize, mostly subconsciously, that throwing more fits will get them more in return. It is better for mom and dad to offer an alternative than to give in to the actual request. If that doesn't calm Junior down, take a deep breath, put on some headphones, and take yourself to a happy place until he calms himself down.

Unfortunately, ignoring the tantrum is almost impossible outside the home. If at all possible, take the child back home. If you are in a situation that requires you to finish your activity before going home, take the child aside and explain why she cannot do what she wanted to do. Other people might stare and point, but unless they never had children of their own, they will be sympathetic to your plight. Again, the key is to remain in control and not to give in. If Junior has a tantrum because you're not buying him a candy bar, he will throw that same tantrum every time you are at the store if you buy him that candy bar.

Don't give in, and eventually the child will learn that throwing a fit will not get him anywhere. Soon the child will learn that throwing tantrums will not benefit him at all and will go the other route: Making himself lovable. ☺

Best Parenting Style Today To Keep Your Family Together

Parenting Magazines and Effective Parenting Views

Parenting magazines generally view effective parenting in two different ways - what ―works" in the immediate moment, or what is most beneficial to the child in the long-term. Many parenting magazines agree that effective parenting usually entails what is the most beneficial in the long run for the child.

For example, a common situation is when a child hits or strikes the parent. Some parents will actually hit the child back, using the rationale that the child needed to know how it felt. Perhaps it might work in the short run because the child will stop hitting. However, many parenting magazines regard this is an example of ineffective parenting because the child never learned why hitting is wrong to begin with. It also does not teach the child compassion. Parenting magazines also contend that it makes the parent look like a bigger child.

Effective parenting has to teach both the parent and the child the long-term value of evaluating the root of the hitting. Why did the child start hitting? Was it out of frustration or anger? Was the child being neglected in some way? Was the child merely testing his or her limits? The effective parent is able to step back and contemplate the situation from a broader perspective. If the child is frustrated or angry, their reaction might be to start hitting. Parents must handle the situation with compassion. Over time, the child will learn that hitting is not the way to go.

It is more important to consider the needs of the child rather than the needs of the parent. At the time a parent is hit by a child, the parent might feel the need to react in kind. There is no benefit to the child to react this way. The child needs the compassion and effective parenting values that will curb this behavior before it becomes a larger problem in the future.

Parents who struggle with a response, rather than a reaction, should allow themselves to calm down before taking action. The old adage —count to ten" is sage advice.

Best Parenting Style Today To Keep Your Family Together

Parenting Skills To Help With Difficult Teen

Every parent has a problem at one time or another with their child. Sometimes problems are easily solved, but other times it takes s a little creative parenting to get the job done.

Every child goes through certain phases, the terrible twos has to be the most popular one of all. After that there is the same sort of phase in the

early teen years.
Here are some things you can try to get past these trying discipline problems.

Tip #1 Hold Your Tongue

Sometimes it is best to step back and not say anything. Your child will see what you are saying as an opportunity to try to talk you out of it. They will argue and they will end up not doing what you want.

Instead, tell your child what you they need to do and the punishment if it is not done. Don't discuss it at all. If they choose to not do it then implement the punishment right away without discussion.

Tip #2 Use The Time Out Method

Have a talk with her before you start giving time outs and explain to your child what you plan to do. It is important for you to stay calm, do not yell and take deep breaths.

If your child does not do what you asked her to do then put her in time out. A child should be in time out for the number of minutes that coincides with their age. For example, a three year old would be in time out for three minutes.
A regular kitchen timer works well for timing.

Tip #3 Keep The Consistency

You need to remain consistent in your discipline efforts.
If you do not keep consistent you will start to lose your battle even if it only happens once. Keep up with this. It does not matter what kind of behavior problem your child has.

Parenting Skills With Discipline

There seems to be a parenting trend going around these days that parents just let their children do whatever they want. This allows the children to be in control, and they know it. They know they can easily manipulate their parents into getting whatever they want whenever they want. This is not a good situation and needs to be turned around as soon as possible.

The older the child is the more difficult it will be because they are so used to getting whatever they want. However, it is important that you put in the time and effort to turn this situation around before things get way worse.

Children should become independent and not need you for every little thing they want. They need to learn how to get it themselves and learn ways to cope with not getting what they want. Here are a couple key parenting skills you can start to use to change things around:

-Start saying no more often. Your children will learn they can not always get what they want and that is a great life lesson.

- Set rules. Rules to follow and consequences for those rules if broken. Show your child that you care about them by setting some rules and consequences should those rules be broken.
Raise an independent, intelligent kid who knows what she wants out of life just by showing her some discipline.

Best Parenting Style Today To Keep Your Family Together

Chapter 17

The Best Parenting

There is no handbook for parenting *(Don't you wish there is?!?!?)*. It is something that is supposed to come natural. It is something that we learn as we go. Each parent has their own way of parenting and learning about parenting. Some people start planning for parenthood as soon as they find out they are expecting. Other people just take it as it comes once the baby is born. There really is no right or wrong way to parent a child as long as the child is healthy, happy and cared for, so each parent has to make their own plan on parenting their child.

One of the most popular ways for new parents to learn about parenting is to **talk to others**. People often talk to friends or family members to get advice on how to be a parent. They may consult older relatives and get age old advice or they may consult younger friends and get some of the new parenting advice. Other people can give their personal experiences and ideas, tell stories about what they have went through. This can be incredibly helpful. An especially helpful part of relying on others for advice is that when a parent needs advice they can simply call upon their friends and family for a little help.

Another method parents use to learn about parenting is **books**. There have been a large array of books written about parenting. Some are focused on certain parenting styles, while others are more general. There are parenting books to suit the needs and style of any parent. There are books about general parenting and specific books about certain parenting topics, like discipline. People like to use books because they are a great reference tool. They often include insight from professionals that make parents feel better about taking the advice, knowing that it is sound and proven advice. As mentioned some people simply just parent. For some people parenting is second nature and they feel they need no help at all to parent their children. It is something that they just do because they were born to be a parent and it just comes naturally to them. They may talk with other parents occasionally or even draw from their own childhood to develop their parenting style. Whatever they do, they largely do it

Best Parenting Style Today To Keep Your Family Together

themselves. They learn from their mistakes and they learn what works. They change the things that do not work and keep up the things that do work.

It is a sort of trial and error parenting, but at the same time these parents know the basics of keeping their children safe and healthy, so their methods never seek to hurt or harm their children, but rather just do not follow any set rules. No matter how much a parent researches parenting they are not going to learn everything until they actual raise a child. Even then, they will walk away wondering what they may have done wrong or what they could have done differently. Parents only get one shot at parenting and sometimes in the rush to be the perfect parent they forget to be a good parent. Children do not care if their mom can not cook anything without burning it. They do not care if dad is not too good at throwing a baseball. What they care about is getting their needs taken care of and about being loved. Children really are not as demanding as one may think when it comes right down to it. They rarely expect perfection. So, parents are actually better off just giving it their best then trying to learn the best way to parent. Their children will never know the difference.

There is no right or wrong way to parent a child. Children need love above all else and as long as their parents love them then they will ensure they get everything else they need. It really doesn't matter where a parent gets their parenting advice or if they get any at all. Parenting is something that is a learning process and parents will learn as they go no matter how prepared they feel they are. Parents will find that children are their own beings and they will always throw something new at you when you least expect it. So, above all else, parenting needs to be full of love, patience and a will to expect the unexpected.

The Best Style for Parenting Today

Parenting today is certainly very different from parenting in the 1950's and 1960's. Although parenting styles remain the same, there has been an emphasis shift as to which styles are more predominant for parenting today.

The permissive parenting style, for example, was very popular in the 50's and 60's. As a reaction to the dictatorships of other nations during World War II, parents took more of a hands-off approach of parenting. This allowed the children to make their own decisions and think for themselves. When the children misbehaved, parents usually did little to correct it. Unfortunately, children raised by permissive parents have trouble in a populated society and have difficulty conforming to rules of the workplace. When misbehavior is ignored, children are given no boundaries as to the right and wrong way to behave. This can lead to aggressive behavior later in life, especially in trying to meet their own desires.

The authoritarian parenting style, too, was popular in the sock-hop era. The —my way or the highway" approach instills in the child that there is only one correct way of doing things - the parent's. This teaches the child that only one authority figure is right and the children have trouble finding their own way. Consequently, some children might fall into listening to an undesirable element, not knowing if it is the correct one.

Parenting today might command more of an assertive-democratic parenting approach. With this style, children are given guidelines for behavior. Although they are given the latitude to make their own decisions and to take responsibility for themselves, they are disciplined appropriately when they cross the pre-established boundaries. Parenting today also involves the parents working with the children in a problem-solving mode in order for the child to learn alternative ways to satisfy their desires. Children who are overly out of control will be given a time-out instead of being punished.

Best Parenting Style Today To Keep Your Family Together

In today's society, where everything is fast-paced and changes quickly, the assertive-democratic parenting style is appropriate. Choices are plentiful today, and it is important to teach the children to arrive at a good decision, as there is more than one ‑correct" way to approach something. Children raised by assertive-democratic parents are able to meet change head-on, can make decisions, accept responsibility, and have the tools to thrive in the collaborative workforce.

Best Parenting Style Today To Keep Your Family Together

Tips For Taking Your Children Shopping

Okay, so you want to go shopping but are dreading going because you will have to bring the kids. For those that have been shopping at a store with children, you know that it can be a very stressful experience, especially if the children or child is young. If you plan ahead, you might just be okay.

Before you enter the store, you will want to set the rules. Make your rules nice and clear. You can tell them to ―Stay close to me" or ―No begging for anything". If you are shopping for someone else, be sure to let your children know, so they don't expect you to start shopping for them. For instance, if you are buying a toy for a birthday present for another child, let your child know this before you even begin shopping. Ask them to help pick out the gift.

Best Parenting Style Today To Keep Your Family Together

If you're in a giving mood, agree to buy them a reward for good behavior. You could also reward them by playing a game at home, watching a movie together, a trip to the park, cook one of their favorite meals, etc. If you think that your child might misbehave, this might be something you might want to try. It has been known to work by many moms and dads.

Depending on their age, you might want to pack a snack or treat for your child to eat while you are shopping. Some nutritious snacks might include raisins, nuts, grapes, sliced apples, nuts, granola bar, etc. Bringing a snack might also prevent them from asking for food while you are shopping.

Other ideas of items to bring with you could be a book for your child to look at or read. You could bring their favorite blanket or their favorite toy. A pencil and paper could also entertain them. The idea is not to go empty handed. Be prepared so your shopping trip is successful and you don't end up turning around and going home.

If your child is hungry before you go shopping, make sure you feed them. This will prevent them complaining they are hungry. If they are tired, have them take a nap beforehand, this will save a ton of stress. The best time to go is when your child has a full tummy and is well rested.

While you are shopping, you can play games with your child to make the trip fun. If you are shopping for food, you can play a game of who sees the bananas first. You can sing songs about what you are buying. You can talk about what is on the packaging. At the end of your shopping trip, let your child help give the checkout clerk the items you are buying. Kids love helping out. Just remember to keep them distracted from the candy isle unless you want to buy them some extra energy.

Best Parenting Style Today To Keep Your Family Together

Universal Parenting Tips

Being a parent is not an easy job for anyone. As such it is not a job to be taken lightly by any means. You are empowered with the responsibility of caring for the kid and also the molding of the personality of a young child. How you do it will determine how the child grow up as an adult.

Remember that all people, including kids, are different. So each family will have different family dynamics and so there isn't a fixed sets of dos and don'ts. Fortunately, there are some universal guidelines by which we can adopt in raising a child.

Now, let's look at a few guidelines which may help any parent no matter who they may be:

Be involved as a parent

Knowing what is going on at school and other areas of your child's life are a good way of making sure they are staying on track. It is also a good way to spot potential problems, such as bullies, trouble at school, or drug abuse. Being involved in school activities and developing a good relationship with your child's teachers can go a long way towards showing your child that you care about him.

Work with the schools

Don't depend on school to teach your child everything he needs to know. Teachers cannot do everything alone. It is important that you help your child study, and that you work with your child at home to reinforce what he/she is learning at school. Make certain that you check homework every night, and let your child know what your expectations are.

Best Parenting Style Today To Keep Your Family Together

Don't punish your child in the public

If your child misbehaves, take him/her to the side and explain what they did wrong, and what their punishment will be. Punishing your child in front of other people will only cause unnecessary embarrassment, which can damage your child's self esteem.

Be firm in your decision

Try not to give in or relent when you have already said no. Telling your child no, and then giving in when he/she throws a tantrum only teaches her that throwing a tantrum is the way to get what she wants. It reinforces bad behavior, rather than teaches good behavior.

Reward good behavior

Acknowledge your child's good behavior and accomplishments. Praise your child for a job well done, and encourage that good behavior. Try to focus on the positive, rather than the negative as much as possible.

Find time for yourself once in a while

It is easy to become overwhelmed when you are with the children 24 hours a day, seven days a week. Have a grandparent or someone help you out once in a while so you can take a break. You will find that your stress level lowers, and that you are in a much better state of mind when you go back home.

Have regular talks with your child

Talk to your child about peer pressure, drugs, alcohol, sex, etc. Let your child know that they can come to you with anything, and that you will help them through whatever problem they may have. Teach them the dangers of smoking, and these risky behaviors. Having the talk one time is not enough, since as children get older, they are constantly faced with peer pressure and put in difficult situations.

Teach responsibility

Teach your children responsibility by assigning chores and making certain they do them. Make sure you give them age appropriate tasks, and explain to them they need to help you by making sure these things get done.

Love unconditionally

If there is anything that you want to take away from this reading, it has to be this statement —Love Unconditionally—Love your child regardless of the results in schools, behavior and conduct. The child needs to know that they don't have to work to merit your love. You love the child because he is YOUR CHILD.

There is a balance between discipline and love. A child may disobey you and set off a fire in the backyard. But you are not going to say —I will NOT love you anymore if you set off the fire again". Instead, you can punish the child with no snacks or games for the week and explain to the child why you conduct such punishment and insist that you did all these because you love the child.

With this, your child will find more security both emotionally and mentally.

These are by far not all of the things that you need to know in order to be a good parent, but these should help give you some ideas maybe you hadn't thought of before. There are many parenting sites online that offer good tips, and forums in where you can actually talk to and seek advice from other parents.

When To Say No To Your Children

I'm sure that many of you who are parents will face the situation where you have to say ―No" to your child. And yes, it can be a tough ―No". Even as they get older, saying no to their wants can be much more difficult. Many parents avoid saying no to their children because they don't want to be considered unfair, mean or a bad parent. Some parents believe that children should have what they want as we only live once and we should be enjoying life to the fullest.

Today, not all parents are able to keep up with the demand of their children. The cost of living is always going up as with the luxuries that we all want and need. We have all these new and advanced toys that come with a high price tag.

It is important that you keep your ground with your children and set boundaries. There will be many times that you are going to have to say no to your child's wants. Giving in to your child is not always a bad thing as long as you keep it under control. It is okay to say yes, but don't say yes every single time. Saying no will help your child realize later in life that you don't always get what you want. Be up front and honest with your child and let them know that you can't always afford to buy them everything they want.

It is also important that when you say no, your spouse will have to stand by your decision. Otherwise, it will deflate the authority of the parent as the child will learn that there is ‑another way out".

When telling your child no when they want something, make sure to let them down in an easy way. Again, be sure to be honest and explain to them why you are saying no. Tell them no in a nice and polite voice. Don't scream or raise your voice unless your child gives you reason to raise your voice. Once you say no, stick your grounds. Don't back down and change your mind. Keeping your grand will give your child a feeling of security which is needed.

If you are able to keep calm, it will rub off good behavior to your children. After letting your child down, offer them something in exchange. Offer them to make their favorite dinner, go to the park, watch a movie, etc. Your child will appreciate what you will offer.

CONCLUSION

The Parent-Teen Relationship:
How Parents Can Make the Most of It

"Enjoy them now, they'll soon be teenagers!" Warnings like this from friends and relatives, together with media images of adolescents as irresponsible, rebellious troublemakers, can lead parents to expect trouble as their children enter puberty. It is a rare parent who does not approach a child's adolescence without some misgivings. But family life does not have to be a battleground during the teenage years. Parents and teens can live together, more or less harmoniously, if parents know what to expect and are willing to make some adjustments in the way they think and act.

The purpose of these fact sheets is to help parents cope more effectively during their children's adolescence. Although this information is intended mainly for parents of teenagers, it is general enough to be useful to parents of younger children as well. The first fact sheet discussed the way teenagers develop and what parents can do to help them through this time in their life. This second fact sheet focuses on strategies parents can use to deal with typical teenage behaviour.

The Cultural Context

Teens get bad press. All too often publicity about teenagers highlights the ones in trouble: the runaways and the lawbreakers. You rarely hear about the hospital volunteers and the camp counsellors. Teens have no status, no recognized place in our society. We no longer need them to do essential chores like milking cows or chopping wood — jobs that gave them a sense of usefulness and worth. (Even when teens work part-time,

Best Parenting Style Today To Keep Your Family Together

their earnings are not usually necessary for their family's survival).

Young people used to grow up quickly. Now we require them to be dependent and regimented until they acquire the education they need to find jobs in a technology-oriented society. Social isolation is another problem. The trend toward smaller families, increased mobility and the high divorce rate often mean there are no relatives close by to help teens and their parents get over the rough spots. When friction develops between parent and teenager, there may be no one to turn to for help and advice, no one who can step in and defuse the situation.

Not surprisingly, parents sometimes feel overwhelmed by the stress of bringing up teenagers. But there are steps we can take to make things better. We can begin by remembering our own adolescence. Asking ourselves questions like "How much did I share with my parents?" "How critical and argumentative was I at that stage?" and "What were my worries and dreams?" can help us accept our teens' behavior better.

Some things are true in every age and in every culture. Adolescence is always a struggle for independence — it is common for teenagers to challenge their parents.

Teens still cope, as we did, with major physical changes, emotional ups and downs, unfamiliar sexual urges, peer pressure, a changing identity, important life decisions and the resulting loneliness and anxiety.

The world is changing rapidly and differs in many ways from the one we grew up in. Teens today face a more complex and impersonal society.

Alcohol and drugs are more easily available. Today's teens also have to worry about AIDS, violence and uncertain job prospects.

The pressures on today's teens are intense. Young people have become a major target group for advertisers and media hucksters, who constantly urge them to grow up quickly and have it all — now!

Family Relationships

Teens are out of balance at the same time as their parents are struggling with their own mid-life pressures. While teens are dismayed by each new pimple, parents may be agonizing over each new wrinkle. While teens are thinking in terms of the time ahead and the opportunities it will bring, parents
are beginning to think in terms of time remaining and the opportunities that are diminishing. While teens are gradually acquiring more personal power, parents are often beginning to confront their own limitations. Giving up power over their children may be difficult. Good parents aim at working themselves out of their job, but the difficult part is knowing how and when to let go.

Parents are not the only ones struggling with mixed feelings. As teenagers try to establish their identity, they have to adjust to the loss of childhood security and accept increasing responsibility. As our children work toward independence and self-control, our attitude to their struggle is crucial to their success. Parents and teenagers will both do much better if parents can keep a sense of perspective.

When parents and teens are getting along, family life can be wonderful. Teens really are enjoyable and energizing. Their wit and high spirits make them fun to be around. But when parents and teens are at odds, the teenage propensity for sullen silence and rejection can confuse and frustrate their parents.

Life with teenagers is an emotional rollercoaster; certainly an adult marriage with so many ups and downs would be considered unstable. Luckily, for parents and adolescents this "on-again, off-again" relationship is normal and nothing to worry about in the long run.

Make the most of the good times with your teens. Think about your children's likeable qualities even when they're temporarily exhibiting their unlikeable ones. It is important for parents to see the instability in the relationship for what it is — a necessary part of the **teen**'s development in separating from his or her parents.

Handling Anger

Growing up is difficult sometimes and anger plays a key part in the process of separating from parents. Teens resent being dependent, but they're afraid of having to take care of themselves. They are annoyed at being treated like an adult one minute and a child the next, but they often behave inconsistently themselves. And then they bristle when you point this out to them. Understanding your teenager's anger will help you respond to it more constructively.

In a society that often appears to condone violence as a way of solving problems, we need to help our teens control their anger and express it safely
— especially their anger at parents. Remember that anger is a normal emotion and that other feelings like helplessness, hurt, frustration, confusion and guilt are often expressed as anger. Ask

yourself: "How can a teenager in our home express anger in acceptable ways? Do we provide our
teenager with any safety valve to blow off steam?" We must make it clear to our teens that yelling, cursing, hitting and other forms of aggression are unacceptable.

There are *non-violent* ways to work off anger: stomping off to one's room, pounding a pillow, twisting a towel, crying, talking it out, writing in a diary or doing some form of physical exercise. In helping teens to deal with their anger, the example we set is crucial.

Like younger children, teens take their cues from us. It is therefore important that we be aware of our own behaviour, so that we don't become part of the problem. Teens often like to bait their parents, and mothers and fathers who overreact can be drawn into a destructive pattern of pointless arguments. The last thing an out-of-control **teen** needs is an out-of-control parent. Mothers and fathers need to ask themselves "How do I behave when I'm angry at my **teen**?

Would I want my **teen** to imitate me?" Parents can work off anger using the techniques suggested above too. When you feel your temperature rising over something your child has said or done, consciously force yourself to back off. Take time out. Give yourself a chance to cool off and relax a little before confronting the issue. It will help you keep things in perspective.

The way you talk is important. In the heat of argument, if you can't help "sounding off" about your **teen**'s behaviour, do it without attacking his or her personality. A practical approach is to start your sentences with the word 'I' followed by a statement of your feelings. "I don't like it when you use that kind of language" or "I'm really upset when you take your anger out on me." This way you will avoid laying blame. In other words, speak as you would be spoken to.

The way you listen is important too in draining off your **teen**'s anger. It can be passive listening — silence is sometimes golden. A more useful way to listen is by trying to understand what feelings lie behind your **teen**'s actions or words.

Your response should start with the word you, as in "You sound like you're pretty frustrated," or "You look like you're really fed up." We all know how important it is to feel heard and understood, especially when we are upset. Remember that you should listen twice as much as you talk.

Best Parenting Style Today To Keep Your Family Together

Teen Depression

What is Wrong with You?

Does this question sound familiar? Do you find yourself frustrated by a teen who seems to have no energy or motivation, who sulks around the house or makes angry scenes when you try to get him or her to "just DO something?" If your teenager has shown a persistent pattern of irritable, depressed, or hopeless behavior for more than two weeks, it may be due to clinical depression.

Unfortunately, many times when parents see resistant, belligerent, or hostile behavior from a teenaged child, they automatically assume this is normal rebellion. Sometimes there is a deeper problem that can be treated and dealt with by mental health professionals. Depression in adolescents can express itself as irritability, hostility, and anger, which can often lead to missed diagnosis. Teen suicide has become a national problem, and it is no exaggeration to say it is an epidemic. The saddest part is that in most cases of teen suicides, parents, teachers, and friends did not realize the child had a serious clinical depression that required therapeutic and medical intervention. We hope that About Adolescent Depression helps educate parents about teen depression, the risk of suicide, and the treatment options

Treating Teen Depression

Of all the worrisome adolescent behaviors that are considered ―normal," teen depression, thoughts of suicide, and feelings of hopelessness are not among them. Adults often dismiss signs of teen depression as normal adolescent angst while their children suffer in silence. But much of the suffering depressed teens experience can be prevented and treated.

Cognitive-Behavioral Therapy Proven Effective

A large study which appears in the June 3 issue of the *Journal of the American Medical Association* reports that positive thinking and coping strategies taught in a cognitive-behavioral therapy (CBT) program help prevent depression in teens.

—We know that these kids tend to interpret situations in overly negative ways," study co-author Gregory N. Clarke, PhD, told WebMD. —The idea is to teach them the skills they need to keep unrealistic thinking from snowballing into full-blown depression."

Other studies have shown that a combination of CBT and an antidepressant medication is more effective for treating major depression than either treatment alone. Compared to study participants who did not receive CBT sessions to challenge their negative thinking:

• Those who received CBT were less likely to develop depression during the course of the study, with about one in five (21%) experiencing new depressive episodes compared to one in three (33%).

• The impact of CBT was most notable in teens who did not have a parent who was depressed at the time, with 12% of these teens developing depression compared to 40% of teens who did not go through the CBT program.

• The researchers estimated that CBT prevented one episode of depression for every nine teens treated – a risk reduction similar to that which has been reported for antidepressants.

Signs of Teen Depression

Common symptoms of teenage depression include:

• Frequent sadness or crying – possibly demonstrated by wearing dark clothing, writing poems or journal entries with morbid themes, or listening to music with dark themes

• Hopelessness – pessimism about the future, failure to maintain basic hygiene, giving up at school

• Less interest in previously enjoyable activities – dropping out of school, sports, clubs, or other activities

• Boredom or apathy – skipping school, low motivation, lack of energy

• Isolation from friends or family – avoiding social gatherings, spending excessive time alone, refusing to talk about issues, difficulty maintaining friendships

• Low self-esteem – feeling guilty, rejected, or insufficient, extreme feelings of unworthiness

• Irritability or anger – lashing out at family members, acting sarcastic or critical, rejecting the efforts of others

• Frequent complaints of physical illness, such as headaches and stomachaches

• Academic underachievement – poor grades, skipping school, dropping out, difficulty concentrating on schoolwork

• Change in eating or sleeping patterns – sleeping all day, staying up all night watching television, gaining or losing weight

• Running away from home

• Self-destructive behavior or comments about suicide – statements of intent to commit suicide, preoccupation with death, drug or alcohol abuse, self-injury or cutting

Not Enough Teens Getting Depression Treatment

Depression can be prevented and treated – the earlier, the better. Yet despite evidence that both cognitive-behavioral therapy and antidepressants help, very few adolescents receive any kind of treatment. A report by the Substance Abuse and Mental Health Services Administration (SAMHSA), suggests that nearly one in 10 American adolescents have experienced at least one bout of major depression in the past year, but only about 39 percent received treatment.

One possible explanation is that teens are worried about the stigma attached to seeking treatment for depression. In a study appearing in the journal *Medical Care* of 368 teens, half of whom had been diagnosed with depression, the most commonly reported barriers to depression treatment were worries about stigma and the reactions of their family members.

"With teenagers, treatment decisions greatly involve other parties, especially parents. For instance, teenagers often rely on adults for transportation. Doctors need a sense not just of what the teen thinks or what the parents thinks, but what both think," study lead author Lisa Meredith said in a news release.

Left untreated, depressed teens are more likely to have social and academic problems, engage in early sex with a higher risk of teen pregnancy, abuse drugs or alcohol, and commit suicide.

Programs for Depressed Teens

A number of specialized programs offer CBT and other therapies to treat teen depression and other emotional and behavioral issues. Programs that take teens away from home for a certain amount of time can be particularly beneficial if a parent is depressed and has created a difficult home environment.

Therapeutic boarding schools offer intensive individual, group, and family therapy while allowing teens to continue their education in a structured, nurturing environment away from home. These private schools employ master's and doctoral level counselors who can help teens develop essential coping skills and communication strategies that will benefit both the teen and his family.

There are also a number of adolescent residential treatment centers that offer a blend of academics, traditional therapies like CBT, alternative therapies like equine therapy and art therapy, and esteem-building activities that reignite a passion for life. In these settings, teens actively work to overcome depression and behavioral issues so they can re-integrate into their families and communities in healthy ways.

Depressed teens tend to grow into chronically depressed adults, causing years of unnecessary suffering and decreased productivity. Don't let depression stand in the way of your teen developing healthy relationships, a positive self-image, and a healthy, balanced life. Depression is a knowable and treatable disease that can be overcome in as little as a few months to a year with appropriate treatment.

Teens Learn Valuable Life Lessons During Recession

Fewer jobs, less money for college, more worries – these are the side effects of a struggling economy that not only affect adults but also trickle down to teens. Although parents worry their teens aren't living the youthful, carefree lives they deserve, there may be a silver lining to the current economic climate: Every obstacle presents new opportunities to learn valuable life lessons.

The Economic Crunch Strikes Teens

There's no question that teenagers are feeling the impact of the economic crisis. According to a survey by Junior Achievement, 33 percent of teens said there seemed to be fewer jobs available, 29 percent said the economy was causing them anxiety, 18 percent say they've lost a job due to the economy, and 15 percent said they've reduced extracurricular activities as a result of the economy. Fourteen percent of adolescents

174 | P e a c e

ages 15 to 17 reported that they contribute money to their family budget, and close to 50 percent said that their parents had discussed family finances with them as a result of the downturn.

Although the news sounds dismal, economists, teachers, and parents are taking advantage of the struggling economy to teach important lessons to the next generation, including:

Living on a Budget. For teens, the recession means spending is out and frugality is in. Jobs once occupied almost exclusively by teenagers are now being filled by adults who have been laid off or need a second job to support their families. Parents are feeling the pinch financially, which results in smaller allowances and fewer handouts. On top of having less money to spend, costs of favorite teen indulgences like junk food or and new clothes are rising, not to mention the soaring cost of getting around with higher gas prices.

Economists have suggested that the current teen spending slump is the worst in 17 years, and the teen unemployment rate is at its highest level since the end of World War II, according to a report from the Northeastern University Center for Labor Market Studies. But the news isn't all bad. Teens are learning how to live on a budget and save money, the **difference between needs and wants**, and how to shop for bargains and make cuts when necessary. Some are getting jobs to contribute to the family income, encouraging teens to look beyond their own wants and become more appreciative of their parents' efforts.

Understanding Personal Finance. The struggling economy also presents teens with the opportunity to learn about economics, the stock market, the fluctuating value of the dollar, and personal investing through hands-on experience. In a few short years, teenagers will be bombarded with credit card offers, student loans, and personal expenses. The current credit crunch may help young people understand the dangers and value of credit as well as strategies for building good credit. Teens can also take this opportunity to learn the basics of personal finance, including how to read a bank statement, create a budget, balance a checkbook, take out and repay a loan, or pay a bill. Learning these lessons now may help the next generation avoid the mess previous generations have created.

Working Through Tough Times. A tightening economy has put a lot of strain on American households. Couples are renegotiating their relationships after losing jobs, their homes, and their plans for the future. Teenagers are looking to their parents as role models for what it takes to get through tough times, which creates a wealth of opportunities for parents to instill values in their kids. For example, it is a valuable lesson for teens to see that life doesn't always go according to plan and that they must remain flexible and have a good attitude even in the face of challenge.

Paying Attention to the Needs of Others. The bad news is jobs for teens are scarce. The good news is teens aren't letting a tough job market deter them. Many are dedicating time to volunteer work and internship opportunities. According to a survey conducted by Harris Interactive, nearly seven out of 10 parents say the current economic climate has made their teens "more aware of the needs of others." In addition, more than half of parents said their teens actively support charitable causes or volunteer with a charitable organization. Volunteer service not only helps on college applications but also can be an excellent way to get work experience, learn a new skill, work as a team, and decide on a career.

Finding Creative Uses for Free Time. Not every teen can afford the newest, trendiest clothes right now, but many have found creative ways to expand their wardrobes by making their own clothes, swapping clothes with friends, or shopping at thrift stores. Not every family can afford a summer vacation, and many teens face stiff competition for a summer job, so they have found alternative ways to spend summer break, returning to old favorites like reading, sports, arts and crafts, and volunteering. Although their stress levels may be high, teens are learning to solve their own problems and get creative.

Life is full of hardship, and today's teens are likely to live through at least one more recession in their lifetimes. What better time than now to learn about fiscal responsibility and discover that life is about much more than designer jeans and instant gratification? No one is happy about the troubled economy, but we can all make the most of the situation by seizing on the teachable moments and sharing a little wisdom with the next generation.

Best Parenting Style Today To Keep Your Family Together

The 'Dos' and 'Don'ts of Parent-Teen Communication

Don't argue with the way your **teen** sees things. Instead, state your own case and speak from that. "I have a different opinion," "This is what I believe," and "This is the way I see it."

Don't talk down to your teenager. There's nothing more irritating than a condescending tone.

Don't lecture or preach. Again, this only provokes hostility. Besides, the average teenager goes "deaf" after hearing about five sentences.

Don't set limits you can't enforce.

Do focus on the behaviour, not the person.

Do think ahead to what you will say and how you will say it.

Do keep your messages clear and concise.

Do stick to one issue at a time.

Rules and Discipline

It's normal for adolescents to try to test the rules. Because adolescents are dependent on their parents for a long time, they can build up a great deal of resentment. This resentment can be expressed by defying parental restrictions. Some rules are non-negotiable — like

"Don't drink and drive" — but keep these to a minimum. Parents who make a major confrontation out of every minor issue risk losing all their influence with their teenagers. In demanding quiet submission, they may unwittingly create a simmering foe. Whenever possible, state rules as guidelines rather than

Best Parenting Style Today To Keep Your Family Together

ultimatums. Otherwise, family life will become a series of power struggles. Parents need to help their children make the transition from parental discipline to self-discipline. For this to happen, teens need to learn how to negotiate and how to cooperate in setting rules and solving problems. Today, as their horizons expand, teens are more often out of our sight; they need to learn how to think for themselves so they can make the right choices when parents are not around.

You can help your **teen** practice negotiating, and redirect energy that might be wasted in power struggles.
Successful **teen**-parent negotiation depends on three things:

1. Involving your **teen** in the process when you make rules, set limits or reach decisions.

2. Keeping as calm and rational as possible even when emotions run high. It is especially important to control your anger.

3. Using the following specific problem-solving method, which helps keep negotiations focused on the issue. Problem solving has several steps:

identifying the issue for negotiation, brainstorming solutions, evaluating and narrowing down the alternatives until you get a solution that you both can live with, making an agreement and evaluating the outcome. In matters of discipline, it is helpful to see inappropriate or unacceptable behaviour as a mistake in judgment or choice that carries consequences for your **teen**. If your **teen** behaves badly, make your feelings known immediately. Expressing sadness or disappointment about your **teen**'s unacceptable behaviour is more constructive than

Best Parenting Style Today To Keep Your Family Together

expressing anger. The former leaves the problem where it belongs — with your **teen** — while the
latter shifts the focus to *you*.

The next step would be to negotiate with the **teen** the appropriate consequences for the misbehaviour so that the **teen** can make amends and be motivated to do better in the future. By asserting themselves, parents project by word and action the message "I love you too much to stand by and see you do something hurtful. When you show me by your behaviour that you can handle things better, I'll back off."
While resolving the immediate issue at hand is important, it's even more crucial for parents to take a long-range view. Their job is to help teens develop the ability to make good decisions for themselves. Young people not only lack experience, but also often have little foresight. Parents should teach their teens to think like chess players: before they make a move, they should try to anticipate the consequences. "What will happen to me if I make this next decision or choice?"

At the same time, parents should be asking themselves "What can I do in this situation to help my **teen** be more responsible?"

Positive Parenting
Growing up is often discouraging. Telling your teenagers "I love you" is less important than showing in tangible ways that you care. One of the best ways is by helping your teenagers believe in themselves. And teens will only believe in themselves if they know we have confidence in them.
Try to recognize their efforts and the good things they do, and reassure them, at every possible opportunity, that they have the qualities we want for them. Give them the message "I don't always understand what is going on with you but I'm on your

side and I have faith that you will sort things out and land on your feet."

Caring for the Caregiver

Our culture is often as unhelpful to parents as it is to teens. Parents are expected to know how to rear their children, and to do a perfect job with very little support.

When our children reach adolescence, we are caught in a classic double bind.
We have to give up control, but society does not allow us to relinquish responsibility. Parents are still held accountable for the behaviour of their offspring — sometimes even after they've left home.

With the loss of power also comes the bittersweet experience of giving up being needed. After years of doing for our children, the fact that they can now do for themselves can bring on a sense of loss. This is especially true for parents who have put their whole heart and soul into childrearing.

You have to take care of yourself through the **teen** years as your children begin to need you less and challenge you more. This means setting aside time, each day if possible, to fulfill *your* physical and emotional needs. This will restore your energy and sense of perspective.

Relationships with other adults are important. If you are a single parent, friends and other parents of teens can be valuable confidants. If you are married or involved with someone, take time out to nurture and enjoy the relationship with your partner.

Marriages can often come under stress during this stage. We need to take care of ourselves and sustain our relationships if we want to provide stability to our teens during this turbulent time in their lives.

Where to Turn for Help

Every parent feels overwhelmed from time to time. If you feel your family life is continually in turmoil or if you are always worried about your teens, you can reach out to other parents, as parents have always done, for ideas and support. You can look for family life education groups or groups for parents with special needs. There is also a great deal of family life education material available in audio, video and printed form. Similar material for people of different cultural backgrounds is beginning to become available. You can also ask your school, doctor or clergy for names of agencies where you can get professional counseling and **parenting** advice.

Suggested Readings

Bibby, Reginald, and Donald Posterski. *The Emerging Generation*. Toronto: Irwin
Publishing Co., 1980.

Brenton, Myron: *How to Survive Your Child's Rebellious Years*. Toronto: Bantam Books, 1980.

Briggs, Dorothy. *Your Child's Self Esteem*. New York: Doubleday and Co., 1970.

Cloutier, Richard. *Mieux vivre avec nos adolescents*. Montreal: Éditions le Jour, 1994.

Best Parenting Style Today To Keep Your Family Together

Falardeau, Guy. *La sexualité des jeunes.*
Un pédiatre raconte. Montreal: Éditions le
Jour, 1994.

Fleming, Don. *How to Stop the Battle with*
Your Teenager. Toronto: Prentice-Hall Press, 1989.

Ginott, Haim. *Between Parent and*
Teenager. New York: Avon Publications,
1981.

Kolodny, Robert et al. *How to Survive*
Your Adolescent's Adolescence. Toronto:
Little Brown and Co., 1984.

Lamarre, Johanne. *Le défi de la discipline*
familiale. Pour mieux vivre avec votre enfant
de 2 à 17 ans. Montreal: La maison
d'édition — Les productions Cognition,1994

Best Parenting Style Today To Keep Your Family Together

Why Teens Say They Want to Learn More About Money Matters

To stay out of debt	88%
To be able to pay their bills	88%
To not have to rely on others for money	85%
To be able to take care of their family	77%
To buy the things they like	77%
To be able to do the things they love	77%
To get a good job	66%
To get rich	46%
To get married	46%

Source: Schwab Teens & Money Survey, 2007

Best Parenting Style Today To Keep Your Family Together

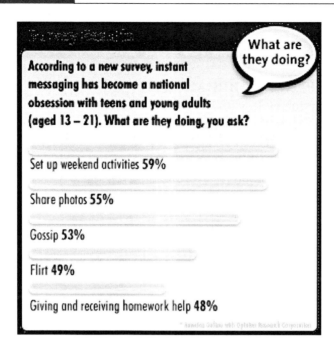

According to a new survey, instant messaging has become a national obsession with teens and young adults (aged 13 – 21). What are they doing, you ask?

What are they doing?

Set up weekend activities 59%

Share photos 55%

Gossip 53%

Flirt 49%

Giving and receiving homework help 48%

Just for Fun Jokes

WOMAN'S PERFECT BREAKFAST
She's sitting at the table with her gourmet coffee.
Her son is on the cover of the Wheaties box.
Her daughter is on the cover of Business Week.
Her boyfriend is on the cover of Playgirl.
And her husband is on the back of the milk carton.
Keep reading-they get better!!!

WOMEN'S REVENGE
'Cash, check or charge?' I asked, after folding items the woman
wished to purchase.
As she fumbled for her wallet, I noticed a remote control for a
television set in her purse.
'So, do you always carry your TV remote?' I asked.
'No,' she replied, 'but my husband refused to come shopping with me,
and I figured this was the most evil thing I could do to him legally.'

UNDERSTANDING WOMEN
(A MAN'S PERSPECTIVE)
I know I'm not going to understand women.
I'll never understand how you can take boiling hot wax,
pour it onto your upper thigh, rip the hair out by the root,
and still be afraid of a spider.

CIGARETTES AND TAMPONS
A man walks into a pharmacy and wanders up & down the aisles.
The sales girl notices him and asks him if she can help him.
He answers that he is looking for a box of tampons for his wife.
She directs him down the correct aisle. A few minutes later, he deposits a
huge bag of cotton balls and a ball of string on the counter.
She says, confused, 'Sir, I thought you were looking for some
tampons for your wife? He answers, 'You see, it's like this, yesterday, I
sent my wife to the store to get me a carton of cigarettes , and she came
back with a tin of tobacco

and some rolling papers; cause it's sooo-ooo--oo-ooo much cheaper.
So, I figure if I have to roll my own .... so does she.
(I figure this guy is the one on the milk carton!)

WIFE VS. HUSBAND
A couple drove down a country road for several miles, not saying a
word. An earlier discussion had led to an argument and
neither of them wanted to concede their position.
As they passed a barnyard of mules, goats, and pigs,
the husband asked sarcastically, 'Relatives of yours?'
'Yep,' the wife replied, 'in-laws.'

WORDS
A husband read an article to his wife about how many words women
use a day.
30,000 to a man's 15,000.
The wife replied, 'The reason has to be because we have to repeat
everything to men...
The husband then turned to his wife and asked, 'What?'

CREATION
A man said to his wife one day, 'I don't know how you can be
so stupid and so beautiful all at the same time.
'The wife responded, 'Allow me to explain.
God made me beautiful so you would be attracted to me;
God made me stupid so I would be attracted to you!

Best Parenting Style Today To Keep Your Family Together

WHO DOES WHAT

A man and his wife were having an argument about who should brew the coffee each morning. The wife said, 'You should do it because you get up first, and then we don't have to wait as long to get our coffee. The husband said, 'You are in charge of cooking around here and you should do it, because that is your job, and I can just wait for my coffee.' Wife replies, 'No, you should do it, and besides, it is in the Bible that the man should do the coffee.' Husband replies, 'I can't believe that, show me.' So she fetched the Bible, and opened the New Testament and showed him at the top of several pages, that it indeed says .. 'HEBREWS'

The Silent Treatment

A man and his wife were having some problems at home and were giving each other the silent treatment.

Suddenly, the man realized that the next day, he would need his wife to wake him at 5:0 0 AM for an early morning business flight. Not wanting to be the first to break the silence (and LOSE), he wrote on a piece of paper,

'Please wake me at 5:00 AM.' He left it where he knew she would find it.

The next morning, the man woke up, only to discover it was 9:00 AM and he had missed his flight Furious, he was about to go and see why his wife hadn't wakened him, when he noticed a piece of paper by the bed. The paper said,

'It is 5:00 AM. Wake up.'

Men are not equipped for these kinds of contests.

God may have created man before woman, but there is always a rough draft before the masterpiece

How to Make a Woman Happy

It's not difficult to make a woman happy. A man only needs to be :

1. a friend	16. a psychologist	32. tender
2. a companion	17. a pest exterminator	33. strong
3. a lover	18. a psychiatrist	34. understanding
4. a brother	19. a healer	35. tolerant
5. a father	20. a good listener	40. determined
6. a master	21. an organizer	41. true
7. a chef	22. a good father	36. prudent
8. an electrician	23. very clean	37. ambitious
9. a carpenter	24. sympathetic	38. capable
10. a plumber	25. athletic	39. courageous
11. a mechanic	26. warm	40. determined
12. a decorator	27. attentive	41. true
13. a stylist	28. gallant	42. dependable
14. a serologist	29. intelligent	43. passionate
15. a gynecologist	30. funny	44. compassionate
	31. creative	

Best Parenting Style Today To Keep Your Family Together

WITHOUT FORGETTING TO:

45. give her compliments regularly
46. love shopping
47. be honest
48. be very rich
49. not stress her out
50. not look at other girls

AND AT THE SAME TIME, YOU MUST ALSO:

51. give her lots of attention, but expect little yourself
52. give her lots of time, especially time for herself
53. give her lots of space, never worrying about where she goes
IT IS VERY IMPORTANT:
54. Never to forget:
* birthdays
* anniversaries
* arrangements she makes

HOW TO MAKE A MAN HAPPY
1. Show up attractive.
2. Bring food

Best Parenting Style Today To Keep Your Family Together

I think you know me!

Best Parenting Style Today To Keep Your Family Together

How should I handle my Teen ?

I won't make duplicat keys for my Dad's Car

Best Parenting Style Today To Keep Your Family Together

Best Parenting Style Today To Keep Your Family Together

"IF YOU CAN'T GET ON THE GRASS, HOW DID THAT SIGN GET THERE?"

Best Parenting Style Today To Keep Your Family Together

Best Parenting Style Today To Keep Your Family Together

Flying Dog

Your are my best friend.

Best Parenting Style Today To Keep Your Family Together

I love you Dad !

NEVER BE AFRAID TO SAY WHAT YOU FEEL

YOU CAN ONLY DIE ONCE!

Best Parenting Style Today To Keep Your Family Together

We are the Team for success!

Best Parenting Style Today To Keep Your Family Together

INDEX

Lightning Source UK Ltd.
Milton Keynes UK
22 July 2010

157332UK00001B/75/P